YLE
FOR
SON
Y
N

R

S

MICHELLE MADHOK

90800100135805

WEAR THIS NOW

ISBN-13: 978-0-373-89259-4

Library of Congress Cataloging-in-Publication Data
Madhok, Michelle.
    Wear this now: your style solution for every season and
    any occasion/Michelle Madhok with Eileen Conlan;
    illustrations by Abigail Smith.
        pages cm
    ISBN 978-0-373-89259-4
    1. Fashion. 2. Women's clothing. 3. Beauty, Personal.
    4. Clothing and dress-Purchasing. I. Title.
    TT507.M347 2012
    746.9'2-dc23

    2011047299

Illustrations by Abigail Smith

www.Harlequin.com

Printed in U.S.A.

CONTENTS

INTRODUCTION: Say Goodbye to the Closet Stare

PART I: SHOPPING PREP

PART II: THE ESSENTIALS
HOW TO LOOK STYLISH EVERY SEASON

9 WHAT TO WEAR TO ALL THOSE FRIGGIN' WEDDINGS 227

10 JET-SETTING STYLE: WHAT TO WEAR ON THOSE GETAWAYS 239

INTRODUCTION

SAY GOODBYE
TO THE CLOSET STARE

As women, we spend an average of *two years* of our lives standing in front of our closets, debating what clothing to put on. Two years! In that same amount of time, you could've graduated from business school, renovated a house, landed your dream job, planned a wedding or done a thousand other more interesting things.

You're not to blame: Not one woman is immune to the closet stare—that moment when you gape at your wardrobe and realize that not one single piece is right for the occasion you've found yourself in. (Men, however, are mostly immune to this. Their version is the refrigerator stare, which occurs when nothing looks good enough to eat—it is much less life-threatening.) The key is planning. We're here to map out your fashion life and prepare you for the events you can't yet foresee. Keep this guide on hand to consult when faced with the most daunting sartorial crises. Think of this book as a crash course in fashion survival, with extremely cool clothes and insider tips for how to score them without breaking the bank. This is intended to be a resource for years to come, helping you build your wardrobe (hitting up sales along the way) and knowing when and how to wear what you've got. The next time you're standing in front of your closet before the big date, the big interview or the night out with the girls, you'll know just what to wear—right now.

WHO WE ARE AND
WHY YOU SHOULD LISTEN TO US

We're editors, writers, businesswomen and, most important, shoppers. We go to fashion shows and market appointments and can spot a trend (and a fake bag) from a mile away. Michelle Madhok is the CEO and founder of SHEFINDS MEDIA, a network of websites for women in every stage of their life, from career-minded girls (shefinds.com) to brides (bridefinds.com) and moms (momfinds. com). The sites are all about how to get the best bang for your buck—and be entertained and get styling ideas along the way.

Eileen Conlan is the senior editor, fashion and lifestyle, of SHE-FINDS MEDIA, which includes shefinds.com and bridefinds.com. She spends day after day checking out the best trends, news and deals available online and sharing them with readers. She was previously a writer and editor at *Marie Claire*, and has toiled away in many a magazine fashion closet, from *Vogue China* and *Elle* to *W*, where, along the way, she learned how to style pretty much anything, from cardigans to belts, and anyone, no matter what their shape.

We are both passionate about making sure you're stylish every single day—we get it, and want you to get it, too, whether you're a fashion beginner or a serious veteran.

HOW TO USE THIS BOOK (PREFERABLY NOT AS A COASTER)

Wear This Now is your go-to reference every time you think to yourself, "I have no idea what to wear!" Whether you've just graduated from college or are considering retirement, this is a universal problem—we all want essentially "magic closets" that can just present us with exactly what to wear now, no matter what's happening. As the seasons change and the invitations flow in—from potentially awkward high school reunions and Thanksgiving feasts to tricky-to-pack-for business trips or dinner with your future in-laws. We'll get you covered, from head to toe, in the chicest way imaginable, 365 days of the year. This is a reference guide you'll check for every closet crisis and use to avoid it. Eventually, you'll get so good at it, you won't even need us anymore. Maybe your closet is brimming with possibilities, but you need help with those unexpected challenges that creep up—you know, the impromptu road trip or meeting your Match.com date's parents for the first time. Once you've soaked up our knowledge and added your own flair (everyone's style is different), your only fashion woe will be what to do with all that time you used to spend staring at your closet.

First, we'll guide you through your closet—whether your "closet" is an enviable walk-in or a makeshift armoire—and help you uncover which pieces work for your body and lifestyle. By following our guidelines, every purchase you make will be a smart one. This book will see you through winter, spring, summer and fall, with an easy-to-follow essential shopping checklist for each season—from a sweltering office in winter to a beachfront resort, to what you should have on hand for a ski trip, a Friday night date, a country club wedding or a black-tie work event, and how to look effortlessly pulled together in even the most treacherous weather.

We'll assist you as you navigate the trickiest terrain. We'll help you dress to impress for every holiday and situation you find your-self in—from New Year's Eve through Labor Day, Thanksgiving, and every wedding, promotion and milestone in between. We'll share the most ingenious shapewear on the market to have on hand for those (let's face it: inevitable) fat days, too, and how to get it all online, so you never waste your precious time sorting through those messy, crowded sale racks. That's not all: As shopping experts, we know which days to shop for the best prices and we'll let you in on our secrets so you can get serious deals. When we're finished with you, your closet will be so well stocked, you'll be able to tackle even the most daunting fashion storms with style and grace.

We believe that shopping should be fun, not just another chore to add to your growing to-do list and that getting dressed should be easy, not a drag. You don't have to have all the money in the world, or a team of personal shoppers—just a little bit of savvy, and some knowledge about what works best on your body. And since every day/invitation/event is different, we're here to help you plan for it all, and dress in a way that is flattering to your particular body type. You'll barely have to think about it.

Ours is not one of those books that tells you that you have to buy a $15K watch to be chic (ahem, fashion magazine editors, we're looking at you). Instead, we focus on how to build a wardrobe with no-fail staples that will work for your body and your lifestyle. Follow our simple rules and checklists, and you'll be on your way to the wardrobe you've always dreamed of. We focus on value and believe in quality over quantity. We'll show you how to work the "Fashion Math" for high-priced items we recommend because they pay off in the long run, and we'll share our easy fashion equations to guide you toward putting together fabulous outfits in a pinch. However, we want to save you money wherever possible, which is why we've included all our outfit-procuring strategies in these pages.

PART I

SHOPPING PREP

{ CHAPTER 1 }

Take a Good, Hard Look at Your Closet

WAKE UP AND SMELL THE KHAKI

Think of your closet as your secret weapon—in this modern era, women not only have more opportunities than ever, more designers at their disposal both online and in-store, but also a million more events to get dressed for. In order to make getting dressed in the morning less of a chore and more of an inherent talent, like breathing, you've got to lay down the foundation. This doesn't mean you have to devote a ton of time—just a little. If you're seriously pressed for time, spend five minutes a day for a week on your closet if you must. We live in New York City, where we don't have the luxury of huge built-in closets or extra rooms to store shoes, which means we have to edit often. Some girls we know use their kitchen to store their shoes—the stove, cabinets and even some refrigerators are packed with clothes and accessories. We like to cook, though, and don't want to risk accidentally broiling our shoe collections, so we're constantly rotating our closets. Even if you have ample space, we recommend that you do this, too. How can you get your wardrobe straightened out if you don't know what you have? You cannot begin without confronting this part. Your closet first needs some serious consideration before you start buying, or you'll end up with some odd combinations of clothes that don't necessarily work together. (This is probably how tangelos were born. The only difference is that they're cute.) Your closet, if you don't cultivate it with care, will be a complete mess. Trust us: We're going to make this fun, and you're going to come out of it looking sexy, confident and sophisticated in the end, and for the rest of your life.

While it can be tempting, after a particularly harrowing day at work, to blow half your paycheck at the nearest boutique on the way home, you won't get the most out of your shopping sprees until you go through your own closet with a plan. So the next time you have a few free hours, take some honest inventory. Haven't worn it in over a year? Does it still look good, and can you think of three more ways to wear it with your current wardrobe? Try it on. Does it look okay as is, and isn't in need of repair? Consider keeping it. If you answered no to any of these questions (and the piece is beyond repair), get rid of it. It may seem hard, but this is the tough love that you need. You'll want to save room for only the pieces that are actually worth it and that add value to your wardrobe. If anything is broken or worn to the bone, it's bringing you down. Fix it or say goodbye.

Start one step at a time, drawer by drawer. This is a much more civilized way of completing this chore—we don't recommend pillaging your closet and making a huge pile in the middle of your room. That's called self-sabotage: You'll never finish if you feel overwhelmed. Trust us: We've been there.

Here we go:

CLOTHING

Look through each part of your closet or armoire. Keep pushing certain sweaters to the back of the closet? Give 'em to your sister or your BFF, who's always borrowing everything anyway. Are your pants pulling across your hips? Don't wait until you lose the weight—they're taking up valuable real estate. Get rid of them right now. You can find another size and style that actually flatters your figure. Other things in your drawers to take a close, honest look at: Tees (are they yellowed or frayed?), leggings (stretched or faded?), shorts or skirts (are they too tight, or can barely button?), sweaters and cardigans (shapeless, missing buttons or in a color you never know what to wear with?). Say goodbye.

Once you've got a pile of discarded items, it's time to play fashion detective: What's the common thread? If they're all cotton button-down shirts that just don't fit you right, maybe that's not your style, or it's time to get a custom one made. If your pile consists of all "dry clean only" pieces you never have time to take to the cleaner, look for pieces that aren't so high-maintenance going forward. If your pile is filled with mismatched prints and colors you got on clearance—things you can't match with anything—you'll know to pass on the sale rack filled with lime-green cardigans next time. In the long run, it's not worth the markdown if you can't make them work with the rest of your clothes.

Ten Items to Toss Right Now

1 **White T-shirts with any holes or stains,** including yellowed underarms. No, you are not allowed to wear them to the gym or even to sleep in; however, you can use them as rags if you must!

2 **Anything with polka dots:** Even if they come back in season briefly, they never last, and more often than not, you end up looking like a five-year-old in them. Don't bother.

3 **Sweatshirts:** You are allowed to keep *one* college sweatshirt for the homecoming game. Ditch the rest.

4 **Light-wash jeans:** They will always make you look fat—it's a universal truth.

5 **Mom jeans that are high-waisted and tapered:** They may be comfortable, but if you've ever seen a makeover show, you know that everyone looks like crap in them.

6 **Sweatpants with anything written across your butt** (especially "juicy").

7 **Bridesmaid's dresses:** Even though she said you could wear it again, you can't.

8 **Free employer T-shirts, baseball caps, sweatshirts (see #3):** No one cares that you were on the 2011 super team marketing launch.

9 **T-shirts that expose your belly.**

10 **Cotton sweaters:** They stretch out and fade. Go for cashmere or merino wool instead.

ACCESSORIES

Now that you're getting the hang of it, move on to your accessories. If your handbags and clutches are still in good shape and you continue to use them, put them all in one place, like a clear storage bin at the top of your closet, or on hooks nearby for easy access. If your accessories are stored neatly and in plain sight, you'll be more likely to use them. If they're in a tangled pile on the floor, not so much. If you haven't used the bag in over a year, take a look at it—is it worth keeping, or has the trendy style already had its heyday? If it was an investment piece, is in good shape, and is worth something, see our eBay tips (in the box on page 11) or store it in the dust bag it came in. Next, go through your belts—do they still fit (without creating fat rolls)? Can you think of new ways to wear them, like with a dress, a coat, or over pencil skirts and cardigans? Hang them up on a hanger or on hooks in your closet so you can see them and wear them often. If not, the Salvation Army or eBay will take them off your hands.

SHOES

Now tackle your shoes—are the boots you wore last season able to make it through another winter? Consider whether you should take them to the cobbler to be re-soled, or if it's time to ditch them for a new pair. Try to get at least two years, or four seasons, including fall and winter out of boots, but depending on how harsh the winter has been they may need to hit the thrift store pile before the next frost. Every woman should have a pair of leather or suede flats, plus comfortable sandals for summer. Flip-flops don't count—save them for the beach. You'll need a pair of boots, a pair of sneakers, pumps for work and a pair of evening shoes. Anything beyond that is a matter of preference, but make sure you've got the basics covered before you go splurging on $625 YSL platform pumps during an online flash sale. Just saying. (For the full scoop on seasonal shoe essentials, see our handy checklists on pages 54, 86, 112 and 145.)

Heels Up!

Use this shoe evaluation checklist:

1 Do they have a pattern, or are they a weird color?

2 Is the heel too high for you to walk in comfortably all day long?

3 Do you get blisters every time you wear them?

4 Are there holes in the soles?

If you answered yes to any of these questions, you really should break your emotional connection to the shoes. There are always more shoes to be worn, and variety is the spice of life.

LINGERIE

Panty raid! Be ruthless in your evaluation of your lingerie drawer. Socks with holes—fix them now or toss them. Ugly or worn-out underwear? You're better than that. Stretched-out bra that isn't even comfortable? Stop torturing yourself and your girls. You can't accurately assess what you need when you've got meaningless fillers taking up your extremely valuable closet—or drawer—real estate. Make peace with the clothes you feel senti-mental about and set them free so someone else can enjoy them.

CASH IN YOUR CASTOFFS

By now, you've culled your wardrobe down to your essentials and you've probably got a healthy pile of items to toss. There's nothing we love more than eco-friendly fashion—especially when going green gives you green in return. Make a tax-deductible donation to the Salvation Army or Goodwill or trade in your rejects for cash at a consignment shop or by selling them online.

Don't be intimidated about selling your stuff online. Here are three easy steps for eBay success:

TO SELL OR NOT TO SELL (ON EBAY)

It's only worth going through the trouble of selling on eBay if the item is expensive, brand-name or vintage. You won't get much for a pleather purse.

Step 1: Find out what's hot

Before you start buying and selling products on eBay, you need to do your research. Find out what's currently hot on the market. eBay even has a spot in its navigation bar for the top twenty-five brands selling in each category. These items sell for a decent amount of cash, and almost always go quickly. Designer handbags are always a safe bet. Fashion is also a decent category to check out, but only if it's a name brand and new or only worn once or twice. Don't go thinking you can unload your seven-year-old winter coat on eBay (unless it's vintage Chanel)—you're not going to get any bids.

Step 2: Take good photos

eBay shopping is about blind trust that the seller is an honest person. Potential buyers qualify this trust by looking for photos that show a lot of detail, so make sure you photograph back, front and close-up. Also be honest about the quality of the item and point out any defects. If you try to hide any damage, the buyer will just be ticked off when she gets it in the mail and mostly likely demand a refund. Not worth the hassle.

Step 3: Charge the right amount for shipping

Make sure you're charging enough shipping to cover your costs. You don't want to get in the situation where the shipping fee eats into your winnings and you can't go back after the deal is done and demand more money. Guesstimate how much the item weighs and then look up how much UPS or USPS is going to charge you to send. If the item is heavy or being shipped internationally, shipping fees can be significant. We once sent a rather bulky overnight bag via UPS and shipping ended up costing more than we got for the actual bag.

Get the Most Bang for Your Baubles

Let's talk jewelry. At a loss for what to do with the mate-less earring or Auntie's tacky cocktail ring? Not to fret—we've got you covered.

Many jewelers have trade-in or trade-up policies. Lots of jewelers will allow you to trade up to larger or higher-quality diamonds, even if you didn't buy your original pieces through them. Take your castoffs and invest in a luxury piece you'll actually wear.

If you've got estate jewelry or other luxury pieces with no definite provenance, you can still make a trade. Companies like Circa Jewels and Portero.com specialize in buying luxury jewelry pieces without making it feel like a pawnshop experience. Get top dollar for your bijoux and put it toward something else that will make you feel fabulous. And, of course, there's always eBay. Let your jewels go to the highest bidder. It's a way better option than just letting them gather dust, hidden away in your jewelry box.

Another solution is to have something new created from your old jewels. If that cocktail ring hasn't fit your finger in years, why not have it melted down and turned into earrings? Or if you lost one earring, refashion it as a ring or a pendant. Most jewelers can do this, so check with your local jewelry shop. Everything you save should always be beautiful *and* useful—no exceptions.

CREATE YOUR SHOPPING HIT LIST

Once you see everything that you own, that you love and that fits you, you can start thinking about what's missing. After the clean-out, look through your closet and think about any time you stood in front of the mirror musing, "If only I had a [something] to wear with this [something]." Write down those things; make a tiered list of things you don't have:

I NEED

I NEED

- ☐ A pair of jeans that fit my body perfectly
  (to wear with blazers, cardigans, T-shirts
  and camisoles)
- ☐ Flat boots (to wear with jeans and dresses)
- ☐ A silky camisole (to wear with cardigans
  and blazers)

I WANT

- ☐ An envelope clutch
- ☐ A sequin mini-dress
- ☐ A pair of sky-high nude pumps
  (they go with everything)

This way, your shopping search will be targeted. Newsflash: You're less likely to spend in complete excess when you actually know what you have and what you actually need to fill in the gaps and make your wardrobe more successful and foolproof for your lifestyle. You won't buy the exact same black blazer or little black dress twice. Want tips for your seasonal essentials? Turn to our no-fail seasonal checklists on pages 54, 86, 112 and 145.

Since we go browsing and shopping online every single day (after all, it's our job), we know you can't just go clicking and buying blindly. Not only is it un-productive and impractical, but it's also expensive. While there's nothing more exciting than receiving several boxes filled with new stuff in just a few short days, you can't really enjoy your purchases unless the clothes fit, and you actually needed them to begin with (and, of course, once the high wears off, have room for them). So you've got to know your sizes. Our advice is to go to a department store. A big one. Bring a pad of paper, or your iPhone to take notes, or even a Polaroid, if you can get your hands on one, like Cher Horowitz from that fashion montage scene in *Clueless*. Be forewarned that many stores don't allow the taking of photographs in their stores, so you might have to do it on the sly using your smartphone or under cover in the dressing room. Try on all the essential pieces you need and want in all your favorite brands, and write down your sizes in each. You're always an 8 in Theory pants? Great; we're getting somewhere now. Perhaps that means Diane von Furstenberg dresses tend to look perfect on you in a size 10, and that J.Crew jeans are best in size 29. So that this doesn't take all day, narrow it down by the brands you really love and buy often; you can always branch out later. Just make sure you have a good base to work with so you can get started.

Email it to yourself and add to it over time, or keep the list in your wallet at all times—you never know when you'll run into a deal. Marvel at your efficiency often.

Five Fashion Commandments to Live By

1 **The right fit always flatters.** Impeccably tailored pieces look expensive and chic, no matter what they actually cost. If you have time to learn how to hem and sew, go for it—if not, strike a deal with your tailor or dry cleaner to fix some of your existing clothes in bulk.

2 **Style and trends are not mutually exclusive.** As long as you know what works for you, you'll always be pulled together—don't feel pressured to incorporate of-the-moment trends into your look if they're not you, or just try them in easy increments, like in your jewelry and accessories.

3 **When in doubt, buy a dress.** Think about it: You're more likely to wear a new dress than, say, a new pair of shorts and a top that can be mixed and matched. Dresses often make more of a statement, and are super easy to throw on.

4 **Your personal style is your calling card.** Celebrities and designers alike have admitted to sticking to a "uniform" of the styles that flatter their own body. Don't be afraid by the connotation: This is not your private school wool jumper we're talking about. Your signature look is what sets you apart from the rest.

5 **Browse often, buy sparingly.** If you know what's out there and see that pieces are marked down every day, you'll be less tempted to buy immediately, leaving room for the stuff you actually want and ending up with only the best in your wardrobe.

RECORD WHAT YOU LOVE

Pinpointing the shapes that you like and that look good on you will make shopping—whether physical or virtual—easier because, quite simply, it's easy to spot a royal blue shift dress from a mile away. Whether structure, like mod dresses, safari jackets, and trousers, works well with your body and style, or if you're more of a flowy, maxi-skirt kind of gal, once you pinpoint the shapes that flatter your particular body and style, shopping will be a million times easier. Scroll down department store websites' long list of dresses and bookmark the ones to that fit your "go-to" list by considering the offerings for about two minutes; your shape-identification time can only have improved since those peg-and-hole puzzles in preschool.

After you've taken inventory of your closet and have gotten a rough estimate of your sizes, favorite designers and shapes, you'll notice some patterns. You buy some things over and over. We've all bought the same little black dress, skinny jeans or white button-down on sale at off-season and completely forgotten about it, only to find it, tags still on, during a closet stare one morning.

You own such pieces, too.

Figure out what they are, and if you're unaccustomed to shopping by pattern, write them down. While your wardrobe should have some variety, there's no shame in wearing the same shape several different ways. Just as long as you're wearing it because it looks damn good on you, not because you're stuck in a style rut.

How's It Hanging?

Here's a trick we use often at the beginning of every season. Turn your hangers around. Then when you wear something, put it back on a hanger facing the correct way. That way, every season you can quickly see what you didn't wear—and say "buh-bye" to those unloved items that didn't get to see the light of day. If you're anal about your closet hangers facing the same way, you can get the same result by keeping your worn clothes on the left side of your closet, or designating different colored hangers.

Take inventory of your body type, too. Every single woman in the world (even Gisele) has some parts of her body she doesn't love to show off.

If your tummy isn't your best attribute, but your legs are, your strategy should be to fill your closet with pieces that will conceal your middle and show off your legs. So you should invest in a blazer, looser cardigans, skinny jeans and leggings, drapey tops, and dresses with some structure, like safari-style dresses, not long maxi-dresses, which will only make you look pregnant. (It's true!) Get yourself some Spanx to suck in the tummy—you'll feel a hell of a lot more confident with a little bit of help in that area. Flaunt your legs: Don't be afraid of skirts, dresses, shorts, and skinny pants or jeans. For winter, stock up on dark tights for all the dresses and skirts you'll be wearing, and get yourself some comfortable heels to play to your best attribute. Now you know what you need to shop for to end up with a closet filled with clothes that work for your body.

Get the picture? Once you do an honest assessment of what your best body parts are, you'll always be dressed appropriately, and your body type will always be flattered. If you've ever witnessed a woman with belly bulge trying to rock a crop top, you can understand why this is important.

Once you've completed your closet clean-out and determined your body type (see page 22), you can accurately assess what still looks good on you. Try on the trousers you haven't worn in two years—if you like the way they fit, you may want to consider getting a new silk top to wear with them. If the pencil skirt you found buried back there flatters your flat tummy, consider buying some turtlenecks or button-down shirts to tuck into it for work.

Rewrite the Fashion Rules

Thirteen Styling Tricks We Love—Try 'Em.

✦ Team statement shoes with show-stopping jewelry.

✦ Pair short skirts with thick tights and sturdy boots.

✦ Temper floral print dresses with neutral olive parkas or leather jackets.

✦ Mix and match slouchy layers with flirty skirts.

✦ If necklaces or earrings aren't your thing, try lots of bangles or chunky cocktail rings instead.

✦ Take playful printed dresses from day to night by changing shoes.

✦ Don't be afraid to pile jewelry on all in one place—bangles, necklaces, rings.

✦ Avoid overly processed hair and bronzers. Go natural—loose locks and bare skin with just a pop of blush.

✦ When layering, try structured blazers and jackets instead of sweaters for an edgier look.

✦ Ditch the ginormous "It" bag in favor of small cross-body bags, clutches or chain-strap purses.

✦ Pair slim-fit jeans with boots and blazers.

✦ Try plaid slim-fit tops with black jeans and flats for daytime dates.

✦ Don't be afraid to add fun embellishments like fur (faux is fine!) and metallic to create interest.

KNOW THYSELF: TAKE A LOOK IN THE MIRROR—AND LET'S TALK

Phew, OK, before you can start taking more of our advice, we have to get down and dirty—and naked. That's right. Take off your clothes, look in the mirror and, without beating yourself up about what you see, take note of what your problem areas are. This will pay off—we're going to tell you exactly what you need for your specific body type.

WHAT BODY TYPE ARE YOU, ANYWAY?

If you've ever picked up a women's magazine, you're probably familiar with the different body shapes. A refresher:

1. Pear-shaped women tend to be bigger on the bottom than on top. You're mainly a thigh-and-butt girl.

2. Apple-shaped women carry weight around their middle with proportionately smaller hips and thighs. You may also struggle to cover a muffin top, which is kind of a cute name for a flabby belly that peeks out over the top of your pants.

3. Hourglass is exactly what it sounds like. Think Marilyn Monroe. You've got breasts, a defined waist and proportioned butt and hips.

4. Rectangle means you're straight up and down—maybe you're thin with very few curves. If you do happen to gain weight, it's not very noticeable, because the fat is distributed evenly on your frame.

BODY BALANCING ACTS: WHAT TO WEAR FOR YOUR SHAPE

The key to dressing for your shape is to balance out the top and bottom halves of your body. Whether you're a size 0 or a 22, we've got tips for what works well for your shape. Here's to a sexier you.

IF YOU'RE AN APPLE

LOOK FOR:	AVOID:
Boot-cut or flare jeans	Low-rise jeans
V-necks	Crew necks
Single-button jackets	Bulky sweaters
Nonskimpy tanks	Ruffles
Wrap tops	Boxy jackets
Empire or A-line shapes in dresses	Body-conscious styles
Sleeveless	Cap sleeves
Slim skirts	Full skirts
Tailored blazers	Shoulder pads
Slim belts	Wide belts

IF YOU'RE A PEAR

LOOK FOR:	AVOID:
Drapey fabrics	Shiny fabrics and sequins on your lower half
Puffy sleeves	Prints on your lower half
Wide necklines	Short tops
Shoulder details like epaulets	Oversized blazers
Wrap dresses	Mini-skirts
Print tops	Baggy tops
A-line dresses and skirts	Pencil skirts
Boot-cut or wide-leg jeans	High-waist pants

IF YOU'RE AN HOURGLASS

LOOK FOR:	AVOID:
Waist-defining belts	Baggy pants and tops
Tops that are nipped at the waist	Pleats or bulky pockets on the hip
Scoop-neck tops and V-neck tops	Tops with big prints or ruffles
Straight-leg or slightly flared pants	High-waist pants
Sheath dresses	High necklines
Pencil skirts	Mini-skirts

IF YOU'RE A RECTANGLE

LOOK FOR:	AVOID:
Higher necklines like crew, polo, mandarin and halter tops	Baggy tops (unless you're wearing them with a belt or some other detailing)
Tops with bust ruffles, ruching, breast pockets and pleating	Clingy tops
Belted jackets, trenches and coats	Cuffed pants
Straight sheath dresses and shirt dresses	Low necklines
Boot-cut and cigarette pant shapes	Boyfriend jeans
Full skirts	Pencil skirts

IF YOU'RE PETITE

LOOK FOR:	AVOID:
A monochrome look to appear taller	Separates
Fitted clothing	Bulky sweaters
Vertical lines	Big prints
V-necks	Crew necks
High heels	Gladiator sandals

IF YOU'RE PLUS SIZE

LOOK FOR:	AVOID:
Wrap tops	Huge prints
Print tunics	Boxy jackets
A-line skirts	Oversized clothing
Platform heels	Empire dresses

HOW TO BUY A BRA THAT FITS, OR CONSIDER THIS YOUR BRA-TERVENTION

Bras are hands-down the most important pieces in your wardrobe. Even though your bra is not visible to every single person you see on the street (unless you're Lady Gaga), it affects your posture, the way an outfit looks on you and even your sex appeal. That's a lot riding on a piece of fabric with underwire and straps. We're so serious about this, it's not even funny: If you're wearing old, shapeless or worn-out bras, you have got to stop. Think of this as your bra-tervention. Not only are they making you look saggy and old, but your clothes

BUSTING A MOVE

To minimize your bust, grab the small-print tops and dresses and steer clear of boxy jackets and blazers. Slim, solid bottoms like pencil skirts are saviors, too. They keep you looking streamlined on bottom.

don't look as good, either. So, rule numero uno: Never buy an ill-fitting bra again!

We know that bra shopping isn't your favorite thing to do. Those annoying flimsy plastic hangers, the sales ladies, the harsh lighting . . . the list goes on. Get over it. Bring your iPod along and make like Cameron Diaz in that *Charlie's Angels* scene when she dances around in Superman underwear. We promise, when you find the right-size bra, you're going to want to dance just like Cameron (though leave the superhero undies to the kids, please). Here are some easy-to-follow tips that will help you get it right the first time. It will take a bit of commitment: All you need is a tape measure, elementary math and some patience, but once you get it right you'll never go back to those ragged old bras again.

Something to remember: Bras are just like clothing—you need to take care of them. Also, bras change over time—and ahem—so does your body. A bra that fit great a few years ago, in all likelihood, is past its prime. Get rid of it. The average life span of a bra is four to six months of daily use. (Interesting tidbit—when men's underwear sales go up, it means good times for the economy are ahead.) Make sure you check your bra size often—life gets busy, but your boobs shouldn't have to suffer because of it. A good rule of thumb if you're not sure whether or not to toss your bras and underwear:

If you wouldn't go swimming in it, it shouldn't be in your drawer. Toss!

FIND YOUR SIZE

This is the life-changing part.

1. Measure yourself at the rib cage right below your breasts. If the number is odd, add four. If it's even, add five. That's your bra width. Easy, right?

2. Next, measure the fullest part of your bust. Subtract your rib cage measurement from this number. You should have a number between 1 and 12.

3. For every inch of difference, you get a cup size. In other words, a one-inch difference is an A, two inches is a B, three inches is a C, etc.

TEST THE BRA

This is the fun part! Use this quick checklist to determine which bra is right for you.

☐ **Comfort:** If you feel any chafing, pressure or irritation, try something else. If you feel discomfort right away, imagine what it will feel like after an entire day of work. Don't talk yourself into a bra that doesn't feel absolutely comfortable at first try.

☐ **Straps:** They should neither dig into your shoulders, nor slip off. Adjust them if necessary.

☐ **Cups:** Floating in empty space? You've gone too big. Spilling over? Too small.

☐ **Underwire:** Make sure it's positioned flush up against your rib cage, both on your sternum and under your arms. If the center between the cups is floating between your breasts or if it's pushing onto the sides of your chest rather than your ribs, you'll need a bigger size.

☐ **Band:** It should fit comfortably at the last or middle notch right below your shoulder blades. If it sits high on your back (or above the shoulder blades), the band is too large.

HOW TO WEAR . . .
A Belt So You Look Like a Lady, Not a Pro Wrestler

We'll be the first to admit that it can be hard to get the hang of belts (they're not just for pants anymore). Once you do, though, there are all kinds of figure-flattering benefits, like a smaller-looking waist and a feminine figure in boxy or flowy dresses. Below, we weigh in on how to wear the four types we think you should own.

WIDE

When your outfit needs a little shape—say, a flowing, formless dress that ends up looking slightly like a sack—select a wide belt to define the curves hiding under all that fabric. Wear a wide belt in a dark hue around your midsection to slenderize, and look for stretchy materials that tend to be more comfortable for wearing higher on the body. We try to avoid letting these wide styles sit on our hips—best to make sure they cinch the narrowest part of your torso. A word of caution: Avoid overly aggressive wide belts, as the size speaks for itself. We wouldn't want you to be mistaken for Hulk Hogan in a world-title belt.

SKINNY

When layering a skinny belt over a cardigan or cinching a dress, aim to place it below your rib cage but above your navel, to create a tiny waist. Since skinny belts are less substantial than wide belts, it's easier and, if you're a beginner, safer, to explore patterns, textures and colors this way. Consider cinching a floral dress with a skinny leather belt to create a subtle contrast.

PATENT LEATHER

Patent leather belts can be both office-appropriate and evening-wear chic—a black one will add some subtle shine and can make almost anything look a little more posh. When wearing a brightly colored patent number, it's wise to stick with a skinny belt, as the color and shiny texture combined can be a little too flashy.

PATTERNED

Eye-catching as they are, patterned belts can cause headaches if not worn correctly. The best way to work the patterned belt is to combine it with neutral pieces. Throw a snakeskin belt over a solid-colored sweater dress, or try a belt that gets its pattern from texture rather than color. Avoid pattern on pattern, though—it could have a dizzying effect on people.

JEWELRY TO FLATTER YOUR BODY TYPE. SERIOUSLY.

Aside from clothing, you should also consider how jewelry works for your body. Sounds crazy, right? Trust us.

✦ **The best earrings for your face:** For earrings, consider your face shape. If your face is oval, you can wear almost any style—your facial proportions are easy to flatter. Choose studs or midlength dangly earrings to show off your shape. Square-faced ladies can soften their angles by choosing earrings with round silhouettes—pearls with their innate spherical shape are usually a good option. If your face is round, stay away from circular silhouettes and try something more streamlined—like dangling rectangles or square studs.

✦ **The best ring for your finger:** If your fingers are long and thin, try a ring with a large stone to balance out the length. If they're shorter and thicker, don't hide too much of your finger with a big rock; instead, try something delicate, like thin gold or silver bands with gemstone chips.

✦ **The best necklace for your body type:** Don't overwhelm a small frame with huge chunky necklaces; opt for a pendant on a thin chain. For curvier figures, choose a more substantial piece in keeping with your overall frame, like a necklace with gobstopper-size beads or a chain with a large pendant.

CHAPTER 2

Shop Like a Pro

Y ou've cleaned out your closet, written your shopping hit list and know what styles work best for your (gorgeous) body. Now comes the fun part—time to hit the stores . . . and the websites. You're going to build a foolproof wardrobe, one sale, one insider secret and one serious deal at a time.

A NOTE ABOUT ONLINE SHOPPING SAFETY

For the most part, when shopping online, there's nothing more to worry about than if you were shopping at the mall. There are some nefarious characters on the internet, however, to watch out for, from fake websites and spyware to counterfeit goods. These are potential traps to avoid. Be wary of ordering from a merchant you've never heard of. If you're ever unsure, just try googling the name of it and see if any bad reviews surface.

If you don't find any documentation but are still wary, you should:

✦ Check the website for contact info—no telephone, no address, no company name? Three glaring clues that something is not right with that site.

✦ Check these sites to see if anyone else has reported a scam:

- ripoffreport.com
- complaintsboard.com
- resellerratings.com

- ✦ Google the name of the website with the words *fraud* or *scam*.

Always use a credit card for online purchases—if a scammer gets hold of your card, under federal laws you'll only be liable for up to $50. Check with your credit card company for more detailed information pertaining to your specific card. Debit cards don't offer the same protection, and a thief could wipe out your bank account. Usually the bank will refund at least some of your money, but only after a lengthy investigation.

OUR INSIDER SHOPPING SECRETS: YES, YOU CAN GET PAID TO SHOP

You don't have to devote your entire life to tracking sales like a crazed, type-A deal hunter on *Extreme Couponing* just to pick up pieces for less. There are some quick and easy ways to do it. Sign up for your favorite stores' email lists. Make a list of the stores you love—if everything you kept from the closet clean-out was from the same store, it's safe to assume you should start there. The next step is to sign up for the stores' email newsletters, follow them on Twitter and join their Facebook fan pages. Retailers frequently give subscribers early access to sales and additional discounts through these social media outlets. You'll never pay full price for the pieces you love again, as long as you're paying attention.

Yes, signing up for all those email alerts is annoying. You can keep them from clogging your inbox by signing up for a free Gmail account, and directing all the messages there. Then, when you *are* ready to shop, there will be an inbox full of savings you can use as your jumping-off point.

EIGHT TIPS TO GETTING THE BEST DEAL POSSIBLE

1. Compare prices.

Always check price comparison websites before committing to a sale. We make it a habit of doing a quick minute of research before handing over the credit card info. Check ShopStyle.com and PriceGrabber.com before buying something in-store or online. An app we love is ShopSavvy—just take a photo of the bar code with your smartphone and in seconds, it'll tell you which store has the lowest price. It may take a few extra minutes, but it's so worth it when you see how much you can save just by doing some extra credit research.

2. Set up price alerts.

This is a biggie. Say you're obsessed with a Burberry trench coat, but you don't want to pay full price. (We can't blame you.) Like magic, you can now sign up to be notified when an item is marked down. ShopStyle.com is a great resource for fashion and accessories alerts. If it's not something you need immediately, or it's something you can live without should it sell out, then it often pays to schedule a price alert and wait for the sales to come to you. This also helps the severely shopping-addicted: You may find that the handbag isn't as much of an emergency after a few weeks—you may even (gasp) realize you can do without it, saving for the stuff you actually want and/or really need.

Use eBay to set up searches, too: You'll get an email when your favorite brands are posted. We have about 20 eBay searches going on at once for our favorite brands and sizes. In the store, we always do a quick search on eBay from our smartphones to check if there's a better deal online. We've even scored Prada snakeskin boots for $50 on eBay. They were posted by a clueless husband who had no idea how much they were worth. This kind of thing happens every day—you just have to know where to look.

3. Visit discounters.
Sites like Overstock.com and Onehanesplace.com are great places to nab a deal on brand-name items from past seasons, store closeouts or refurbished electronics.

4. Shop off-price stores.

We've scored big deals at off-price stores like Loehmann's, Filene's Basement and T.J.Maxx. These stores have the same brand names and styles that are in department and specialty stores right now, but for up to 60 percent less. Never, ever, pass up a really good bargain if you know you'll get good use out of it. Off-price retailers receive limited quantities of each item, so merchandise can sell out very quickly. That perfect dress or handbag may not be there the next time. Take it home to think about it. If you change your mind, the stores have liberal return policies.

Early-Bird Special

If you're going to shop an off-price retailer, go first thing in the morning when the store opens. Discount stores tend to get disheveled quickly, and are often understaffed on the floor, so you want to go when the racks are still organized and your dream dress isn't hiding in the dressing room. If you happen to be there during the day, always check the end of the racks and the discard rack outside the dressing room. That's where good shoppers tend to dump their rejects—one woman's trash is another woman's treasure!

5. Don't be promo-phobic.

To find promotional or coupon codes for extra savings online and free shipping, go to RetailMeNot.com or simply Google the name of the site with the words *coupon code* or *promotion code*. If you use Google, though, be prepared for a lot of spammy sites with expired coupons—it helps to include the month and year you're looking for to filter them out. We like to use RetailMeNot.com because it's a "crowd-sourced" site, meaning hardcore deal seekers post coupon codes they've used and reviews that include whether or not they actually worked. This way you don't have to try a ton of codes just to get the right one.

We've saved anywhere from $10 on shipping to $200 on a pricey winter coat, so it's definitely worth hunting down those codes.

6. Get cash back.

If you're going to be shopping online anyway, you might as well get a kickback. Websites like Ebates.com, Mintbox.com, MyPoints.com and HooplaDoopla.com will give you a small percentage back on everything you purchase. They partner with most major retailers, so there's really no downside to paying them a visit before checking out. Some credit card sites do this, too, so check out who's giving the biggest percentage back before you commit to purchasing. The percentages range from 1–20 percent, with most falling in the 1–4 percent range. It might not seem like much, but if you're doing a lot of shopping, it can add up to some nice refund checks. The refunds will either show up automatically on your credit card, in a check or in your PayPal account, depending on your selection. Most payments are paid out every three months. The sites also frequently offer special coupons that you can use and still get the rebate.

7. Leave the item in your cart.

When shopping online, if you don't check out right away, you may receive a follow-up email offering a discount. Warning: The price might also go up or the item may sell out. It's a gamble, but it can be totally worth it if you get a great price.

8. Buy discounted gift cards from your favorite stores.

Sites like Cardwoo.com and PlasticJungle.com sell gift cards at 9–20 percent off. So if you find yourself shopping repeatedly at one store, it pays to prepurchase these gift cards to have on hand—for *yourself*. A $120 gift card may be listed for as low as $50 just because someone wants to get it off her hands—free money! Obviously, this is also a sneaky money-saving tip if you buy gift cards for the holidays, too. Nobody has to know.

WORK THE SEASONS TO GET A DEAL: TEN PERCENT OFF IS NOT A SALE—IT'S A TAX CREDIT

GOING, GOING, GONE

- - - - - - - - - - - - -

Some websites will tell you the quantity of items that are left in stock. That way you know if you need to buy now or can wait a while. Some of our favorites include Shopbop.com, Amazon.com, Bluefly.com and TheOutnet.com.

There's nothing like that shot of adrenaline when you get a great price on something that would normally drain your wallet. The love of our life is a price tag covered in markdowns. The key to seasonal steals is to shop on the cusp of every season, and even to do some strategic off-season shopping—we've found the most unbelievable deals this way on pricey winter items, especially for those big-ticket winter accessories that cost a fortune, from coats and boots to hats, sweaters and gloves.

Most serious sales occur toward the end of each season, but markdowns can start just a month or two into the season. Floor space is limited, and stores need to move the seasonal merchandise to make room for the new trends of the upcoming season. (Same goes for the farmers and their crops, by the way.) These sales are the best time to stock up on items you wear a lot, like T-shirts or tights, or covetable big-ticket items like winter coats and boots. But don't just buy them because they're on sale: Get the cream of the crop.

End-of-season sales usually last for only a few weeks—sometimes even less. The longer you wait, the deeper the discount, but again, the item you've got your eye on could sell out in your size fast, so beware! (If your shoe size is an 11, or a 6, however, you're probably safe—the less common sizes are often left over and therefore, are more likely to be found on the sale rack. But if you're a 7.5, you should probably buy the pair you love now, or risk losing them forever.) Some items, like jeans that were once only discounted 10 or 20 percent, may be marked all the way down to 70 percent by the end of the sale. This is where you have to survey the landscape and decide when the best time is to pounce on the deal. If there are only a few items left in your size, go for it, but if they've got racks and racks, lie low and check back in a week to see if the price drops even further. If you decide to go even further and make friends with the salespeople, they will frequently tell you when the next price drop is coming, so you can decide whether it's worth waiting. To do this, begin by being genuinely friendly and easygoing to start, and gradually build a rapport. To remind you, at the beginning of each seasonal chapter we'll tell you what to watch for on the sale racks so you can get the pick of the litter.

Hump Day = Hell of a Deal Day

Stores tend to run sales midweek, when they have less foot traffic. A big way retailers draw in customers is to offer incentives, like promos, free shipping and the like on their slowest days. Banana Republic, The Outnet.com and JCPenney, for example, tend to offer discounts each Wednesday. If you subscribe to store newsletters and follow them on Twitter, you'll start to learn the patterns. The moral of the story is that no matter what, everything goes on sale eventually. Even Chanel.

Other retailers are known for their annual sales, and will gladly let you know when to start looking out for them: American Apparel puts all swimwear on sale in June; Bare Necessities features holiday sales for President's Day, Memorial Day and Labor Day; and Nordstrom always has a blowout Anniversary Sale (which includes new fall merchandise like coats and boots) at the end of July, to name a few.

Spring cleaning season in April and May is the best time to hit up consignment and thrift stores. Head to wealthy neighborhoods to score never-worn or gently worn castoffs at a fraction of the price. Consignment stores are an excellent place to grab designer handbags at a discount as well—something to keep in mind if you have champagne taste on a beer budget.

OUR FAVORITE HUNTING GROUNDS

When we are seriously shopping, we're out to seek and destroy—getting the best item for the best price, as quickly as possible. And that means knowing which store carries your sartorial prey.

LUXURY HANDBAGS

Portero.com	TheOutnet.com
eBay.com	Consignment stores
Vivre.com	

HIGH-END SHOES

Off 5th Outlet	DSW.com
Neiman Marcus Last Call	Couture.Zappos.com

UNDERTHINGS

BareNecessities.com	Target.com
OneHanesPlace.com	

T-SHIRTS

J.Crew	eBay.com
Gap	

DENIM

Piperlime.com	Loehmann's
T.J.Maxx	

IF THE SHOE FITS . . .
PUT IT IN YOUR CART

Shopping for shoes online can be a very tedious and nerve-racking experience. What if they don't fit or they looked one hundred times better on the website than in person? In addition, many companies require you to pay shipping both ways if you decide to return them, which means more money down the toilet and hours wasted standing in line at the post office. Use these tips for stress-free online shoe shopping:

1. KNOW YOUR SIZE. Keep track of how different brands fit when shopping in-store.

2. READ THE REVIEWS. There can be valuable information there from other users about whether or not the shoes fit true to size.

3. GET FREE SHIPPING. Some of the most notable retailers that provide free shipping are Zappos.com, Onlineshoes.com, Piperlime.com and Shoes.com. Many other online retailers will offer free shipping periodically with other promotions—sign up for store newsletters or follow them on Twitter to avoid shipping costs.

BE KNOCKOFF SAVVY

No seller on eBay or Amazon is going to tell you the designer item you're about to drop upwards of $100 for is not authentic. Nope, if everyone is to be believed, every Jimmy Choo out there in the internet marketplace is the genuine article. Unfortunately, that's not the case. We've heard horror stories of counterfeit Marc Jacobs bags, fake Tory Burch flats and shoddy "Diane von Furstenberg" wrap dresses. Follow our guide to fakes to make sure you're not one of the unlucky ones who end up with faux fashion.

1. SHOW ME THE PHOTO. Look for sellers who show photos of the actual item that's on the auction block. If the seller only uses a stock photo of the item or a photo of a celebrity wearing the real deal, chances are you'll wind up with a fake. When it comes to bags, get as many pictures as you can of the actual bag you'll be purchasing. Tiny subtleties, like the shapes of certain letters and the colors of trim, thread and canvas can give your bag away as being fake.

2. TRY TO GET AN ORIGINAL RECEIPT. You can email the seller—if you have a paper trail and the sale doesn't pan out, you can get the retailer on your side and get your money back. If your bag was originally purchased "in bulk" or from suppliers or side-door merchants, steer clear.

3. KNOW HOW TO SPOT QUALITY CRAFTSMANSHIP.
Sloppy stitching is a dead giveaway. A bag with stitch lines that look like they were stitched by someone who had one too many martinis—even in the less visible areas—is a red flag. Metal grommets should be polished and tight to the fabric (fakes, which are made quickly, will often have shredded canvas poking out from beneath loose grommets). Stitching should be clean and uniform, with no frayed edges or loose loops.

4. DO YOUR RESEARCH. Run a search for the item you want to buy in the "reviews and guides" section of eBay and read multiple reviewers' takes before dropping your money on what you think is an original. Some of these reviewers have taken magnifying glasses to the good, the bad and the unforgivably fake items, and their findings are documented thoroughly online.

5. DON'T BUY INTERNATIONAL. It may be tempting to get a seriously cheap item from China, but while you may dream of an inside deal from the factory, what you'll receive is a cheap imitation.

Now that we've told you all you need to know to be a savvy shopper, you're ready to start crossing items off your list of essentials. Read on for the full scoop on seasonal essentials and occasion-specific necessities.

PART II

THE ESSENTIALS

HOW TO LOOK STYLISH EVERY SEASON

CHAPTER 3

Your Ultimate Winter Wardrobe

December. January. February. (And, let's face it, we're freezing our asses off in March and sometimes April, too.)

THE STRATEGY:
WHAT YOU NEED FOR WINTER

Out of all of the seasons, winter drags on the longest and can be the most predictable (wind, snow, sleet and more wind), so it's especially crucial for you to get the pieces you'll really need.

These pieces are going to work harder than any in your closet. They've got to be warm, chic and functional—a tall order, but completely doable. From the most frigid days to the most opulent parties, the snowiest vacations, and all the chilly days in between, here's your list of essentials so you'll be covered every single day until (ahh!) spring.

YOUR WINTER HIT LIST

- ☐ A heavy wool or cashmere coat (bonus points if the lining is patterned or fur)
- ☐ A waterproof jacket
- ☐ An array of tights for different occasions—opaque, wool, cable knit
- ☐ Several well-made cardigans, basics for work and dressier ones for parties
- ☐ Cashmere sweater(s)
- ☐ Layering tanks
- ☐ A great pair of skinny jeans to tuck into boots
- ☐ A wool pencil skirt
- ☐ A fun cocktail dress or embellished skirt
- ☐ Silk shells for layering
- ☐ Long-sleeved shirts or turtlenecks in neutral colors for layering
- ☐ At least one tailored, long-sleeved sheath dress
- ☐ A cocktail ring or statement necklace
- ☐ A white button-down shirt
- ☐ An amazing pair of flat boots
- ☐ Rain boots that don't look like rain boots (see page 94)
- ☐ Black wool pants in a shape that flatters you (see the box on page 23)
- ☐ Jersey leggings for lounging
- ☐ Several pairs of cashmere socks
- ☐ Sunglasses

- [ ] Slippers
- [ ] Leather or suede gloves (even better if they're lined in cashmere or fleece)
- [ ] Silk long underwear
- [ ] Fingerless gloves if you're attached to your iPhone or iPad
- [ ] A cashmere or merino wool hat in black or another neutral color

WHAT'S ON SALE NOW

January is the time to score holiday leftovers, and we don't mean from dinner. Gloves, scarves, hats—anything easily boxable and one size fits most that didn't end up under the tree will be seriously price slashed come January. January is also the time when workout gear goes on sale to give you something to wear as you fulfill that New Year's resolution. In February, you can find deals on puffy coats and those boots you've had your eye on. Around Valentine's Day, many lingerie companies offer deals, so if you need to refresh your top drawer, this is a good time, especially after the holiday. Come mid-March, most winter items will be cleared from the floor to make way for spring, so don't wait too long to stock up on your winter essentials.

AFTER DECEMBER 25, WATCH FOR SALES ON:

- - - - - - - - - - - - -

Jackets and winter coats
Scarves
Sweaters
Hats
Boots
Jewelry
Faux and real fur
Fall and winter handbags

Yes, They *Do* Exist . . .

Save your jeans from getting ruined by snow and salt when you're wearing flats by temporarily shortening hems using these cool hem adjusters. (So brilliant, of course women entrepreneurs invented them!)

1 **Hemming My Way.** These four adhesive plastic strips snap under your jeans when you're wearing flats, and then unsnap so you can wear your jeans with heels, too. The snaps work with wide-leg pants and straight-leg jeans, plus, they're machine-washable and reusable.

2 **Zakkerz.** These temporary roll-up wraps secure pants that have been rolled up to a shorter length for flat shoes. You just roll your pant leg up to the desired length, then wrap zakkerz around the bottom of each pant leg with one end inside the pant leg and other end outside the pant leg. The magnets bring the two ends of the zakker together, holding the roll-up in place. They might not be the most fashionable things in the world, but they will keep your expensive slacks and jeans from an early trip to the trash and will save you from having to buy new pairs more often.

3 **City Clips,** which also work using magnets, have gold-plated buttons and other embellishments that let you cuff trousers so you won't step on them during your commute to work.

HOW TO ORGANIZE
YOUR CLOSET FOR
~~HIBERNATION~~ WINTER

First, store away all your summer clothes (except camis and tees you plan to layer) and make room for your arsenal of heavy attire. Stack all your sweaters, leggings and pants on shelves. Hang your work clothes together—your button-down shirts, skirts, trousers, blazers and dresses. Make your cold-weather accessories easy to reach by storing your hats, scarves, gloves and umbrella in a clear bin or basket. As for shoes, keep your boots together—same goes for pumps, flats and slippers. The easier to grab and go.

FINDING THE PERFECT
WINTER COAT

No matter what climate you live in, your coat is your armor against the cold. In no other season do you wear the same thing every day, so put some thought into it.

SIZE

Bring a heavy sweater you wear often with you when you're trying coats on so you can get an accurate feel for what it will look like with your actual winter clothes on. There's nothing worse than having a coat that you can't fit your sweaters under—what's the point? The front should be smooth, and your body should look streamlined, not like a stuffed sausage. Try not to be too worried about the size number and just pay attention to how comfortable it feels. You're going to be wearing it for months to come. We have both made the mistake of buying winter coats during a great off-season sale in the summer, only to find it was too snug after indulging in too many late-night macaroni and cheese binges come December. Shop wisely: If you tend to gain a few pounds with the cold weather, don't buy your coat while it's bikini season—or just go a size up to be safe.

**FASHION
FLASHBACK . . .
LE SMOKING JACKET**
- - - - - - - - - - -
Yves Saint Laurent put a sexy spin on menswear in 1966, changing the world of fashion forever. This perfect little tuxedo jacket spearheaded what would later become the "power suit." If you don't know what to wear for nighttime on, say, New Year's Eve, or any other special night out in winter, when it's way too cold to wear a dress, this is your answer. It is always chic, and the more tailored the better. Try a sharp shoulder or a cool fabric like velvet or leather trim for a fashion-forward look.

COLOR COATED

Decide first if you want to stand out or blend in. Personally, we think a brightly colored coat in winter or one with a print is fun and festive, and tweed with ornate buttons or toggles can look fresh, but it might not be appropriate everywhere, so consider the types of events you have coming up before you invest. We love the look of ivory-colored coats—winter white is so beautiful, especially in a sea of black coats—but if you hate going to the dry cleaner or put your coat through the ringer each year with city grime and commuting, this one probably isn't for you. If you only plan on wearing one coat this season and you're sick of plain old black, you may want to consider camel, chocolate, emerald green or sapphire, gray or olive. If you absolutely must wear a black coat, consider a herringbone, bouclé, houndstooth or other texture to break things up a bit. Insider tip: Textured coats are better to hide fuzz and other debris that can end up accumulating during winter months.

Ditch the Pea Coat: Four More Styles You Should Consider

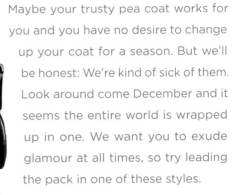

Maybe your trusty pea coat works for you and you have no desire to change up your coat for a season. But we'll be honest: We're kind of sick of them. Look around come December and it seems the entire world is wrapped up in one. We want you to exude glamour at all times, so try leading the pack in one of these styles.

1 **Funnel neck coat.** With a high neck, you'll get more coverage, and it creates a long line, making you appear taller.

2 **Toggle coat.** Perfect for daytime, the toggle is a traditional British style that can be very cute, and is sometimes lined in plaid flannel, keeping you extra warm.

3 **Zip-up, A-Line coat.** We love this style, especially in a bright color, like red or blue. Easy to get on and flattering to most figures.

4 **Belted coat.** While it can be a hassle to belt your coat every time you put it on (not for girls constantly in a hurry), we still love the look of this, especially in jewel tones, like emerald green, for evening events. You can always add your own leather belt to any coat, too, which is a very stylish (not to mention more personalized) look. The better to grab it from the coat check unscathed!

DETAILS

Hoods are a wonderful creation. If it's especially cold in your region, it may be worth it to invest in a coat that has one attached. If you like an opulent look, fur or faux fur could be your ticket—whether on the lining of a hood or at the sleeve cuffs. We like the contrast of an anorak-style army coat with a fur hood, too—even better if it's lined inside as well. You may never want to take it off.

LINING

If your coat is lined in satin or a bright color or print, not only will it keep fuzz from the sweaters you're wearing underneath at bay, it'll also be more easily identified after a party, making it less likely that someone else will walk away with your coat. It's happened to both of us—chalk it up to good taste. Now we're both suckers for coats with linings—it helps distinguish the coat and makes it appear more finished anyway. Conversely, if you own a coat with a lining that's ripped, bring it to the dry cleaner to get it fixed right away. It's highly likely someone will catch a glimpse of it and it will actually work against you at, say, a job interview, discounting all the research you did to prepare for the job in the first place. For more interview tips, see page 198.

HOW TO WEAR . . .
Tweed, without Looking Like Granny

Don't be afraid of the traditional tweed—use it to add texture to your outfits. To modernize the look, opt for:

1 Tweed coats in monochromatic colors like dark gray (the better to hide dirt) with vibrant, colorful prints like florals, graphics and watercolors.

2 Shorter tweed jackets, belted at the waist, with a skirt, tights and flat boots or pumps.

3 Tweed pencil skirts with a tucked-in crew-neck sweater or top, plus pumps or high-heel boots.

Grandma who?

MATERIAL

Warmth is key. Make sure you get something that feels super-cozy. By all means, don't cheap out on your coat—you'll regret it during those unforgiving January days. Wool blends are everywhere and are very warm. Cashmere is extremely soft and warm, but it's delicate and can pill easily. Plus, it requires many more trips to the dry cleaner, which can add up in the end, and can be inconvenient. If you're set on cashmere, consider a coat with cashmere lining or piping as an alternative, or, at the very least, one in a darker color to hide stains.

Wearing Rain Boots in the Snow

If you get an amazing pair of rain boots, you don't actually need another pair of winter boots, especially if you live in a place where you don't get hit by blizzards very often. See our list of rain boots on page 97, and then add a warm fleece liner—Hunter makes great ones. Slip them into your rain boots and you're good to go: You just saved yourself another trip to the shoe store.

FASHIONMATH:
Is a Fur Trapper Hat Worth the Cost?

Let's talk investments. Every year, as much as you want to deny it, it happens: It gets really cold. Instead of being surprised each time, and buying a new hat each year, get one that actually stands the test of time. In my experience, the same old knit black hat I buy every year is a terrible investment: I lose it when it gets dark out, and it's not even that warm. A fur trapper hat (the one we're currently lusting after retails for $279), though, is serious. Between the soft fur, the ear flaps and the thick lining, we're warm just looking at it.

But when that first snowfall hits, you won't regret dishing out the dollars for this hat. The real question—is the fur worth the funds? We break it down . . .

$\left\{ \begin{array}{c} \textbf{\$279 divided by 58 warm days =} \\ \textbf{\$4.81/wear} \end{array} \right\}$

If you wear this hat three or four times a week until February, it equals less than the salad you're about to buy for lunch. But feel free to wear it next year and the year after. You can pair this hat with other faux fur accessories or just a cute winter scarf. Either way, we know where our money is going—how about yours?

Nice Coat, Ms. Michelin: Try Some Puffy Options That Don't Make You Look Like a Marshmallow

Michelin Man coat? Bad. Warm coat that still shows your curves? Good. For those in need of a demonstration, behold the dos and don'ts of donning winter's favorite puffy jacket. Who wants to spend all that time at the gym if your new-found coat makes you look three times bigger than you are?

- ✦ Go for a dark color. Black is always chic and slimming, but we don't have to tell you that.

- ✦ Get a tailored fit. Long lines and plenty of warmth are great, but not if the coat is wearing you. Think slim-cut.

- ✦ Look for a coat with multiple quilted segments. This will help you avoid being puffy all over. A belt gives the impression that you still have a figure under all that polyfill.

HOW TO WEAR . . .
Thigh-High Boots,
without Looking Like a Hooker

Thigh-high boots are at once sexy and warm and can be an ultimate fashion "do" for winter. But wear them the wrong way and you've got a terrible fashion "don't" on your hands. Here's the scoop on how to work them without looking like you're, um, *that* kind of working girl:

- ✦ Keep tights or pants dark and solid. Patterns and textures will draw the eye right to the largest part of your thigh.
- ✦ Try solid tunics, mini-dresses or form-fitting sweater dresses.
- ✦ Stick with one or two color families so you look pulled together, not like a mess.

BUY BOOTS THAT FLATTER YOUR BODY

There are tons of boots on the market, and retailers are finally hip to the fact that not everyone has model-size calves. Whether you're athletic or plus-size, here's how to find a pair of boots that fits your legs. Instead of wrestling with your potential pair of boots, commit to a try-on session and consider going up a size. You might find this makes all the difference. Bring along a pair of thick socks—which, let's face it, in winter you'll be wearing anyway. This will help keep your feet comfortable and helps make up for the size jump. Another option is to try boots with a stretchy leather for more give. If these tricks don't work for you, see if there are any booties that strike your fancy. You might just find you like them better after all.

BOOT CAMP: FIVE BRANDS THAT MAKE THE COOLEST BOOTS

- - - - - - - - - - - -

Frye

Kelsi Dagger

Ralph Lauren

Kenneth Cole

Jimmy Choo

FASHIONMATH:
Are High-End Boots Worth the Splurge?

Every year, we find ourselves drooling over tall leather boots in gray. There's just something about the cool, goes-with-everything gray color, and the rich leather that screams "NEED!" Not to mention the fact that leather boots will outlast your faux leather cheap ones by several seasons. The pair we currently love retails for a whopping $695. But how to justify? Are these flat boots with a three-digit price tag worth it? Let the fashion math speak for itself:

{ **$695 divided by 156 days of fall and winter walking = $4.46 per wear** }

If you wore these boots for three days of every week from October until April for the next two years, these almost $700 boots come out to less than $5 per wear. Let's face it, your lunch is probably more expensive. And you can't put a price on the hundreds of compliments you're going to get, as well as all the new outfits in your closet. Not to mention you'll definitely wear them more than three days/week anyway. Worth it.

SEASONAL SOS

Don't let the sleet, snow and cold weather compromise your style. Here are your solutions for winter's worst fashion emergencies so that you look good and feel good—no matter what the forecast.

SOLUTIONS FOR WINTER
FASHION EMERGENCIES

Common cold-weather annoyances can be easily solved by a few ingenious products we've found. You'll wonder how you ever got through winter without them.

1. The gaps in your scarf let snow/sleet/rain in and leave you shivering.

SOLUTION: Infinity scarves (also called "snoods") are knit in a continuous loop, so they cover your entire neck and then some. Plus, you never have to worry about tying them—simply loop the scarf around your neck. The slouchy, cozy look is always in style.

2. Snow, sleet or freezing rain seeps into your rain boots.

SOLUTION: Removable fleece liners you can toss in the wash without a hassle. Hunter and many other rain boot companies make these in tons of colors— simply slip them into your rain boots—you'll be warmer and they're less expensive than buying a new pair of winter boots. Bonus points: They make great stocking stuffers because they're little indulgences you wouldn't think to buy yourself. Who wouldn't love a pair?

3. You shy away from wearing dresses and skirts in freezing weather—it's simply too cold for tights.

SOLUTION: Fleece tights. According to *Women's Wear Daily*, women from Chicago alone are practically keeping the company that makes them, aptly named Plush, in business. They're cozy and warm—kind of like wearing leggings but without the added bulk. Take our word for it and grab a few pairs at the beginning of the season—they sell out faster than you can say "winter storm watch."

4. You worry about your expensive heels getting ruined by salt on the streets and potentially snowy weather.

SOLUTION: Shoe Slickers are like ponchos for your feet. Slip them into your purse—they're lightweight and under $5. A great investment, if you ask us. And though they're not exactly attractive, they're perfect in a pinch—and better than going barefoot in the snow.

5. You were changing after work for your umpteenth holiday party and got deodorant streaks all over your little black cocktail dress.
SOLUTION: This happens to us all the time. Luckily, Gal Pal Deodorant Remover pads soak up the chalky mess in just a few minutes. Store them in your bag—they're as light as a small sponge, and under $10.

6. Your knee-highs flop. When your boots are bent and strewn around your closet floor you're bound to get unsightly wrinkles in the leather.
SOLUTION: The adjustable, plastic Boot Shaper helps boots stay upright when you're not wearing them, keeping the cracks and creases out of the leather or vinyl, while the nifty hanger allows for easy boot storage in and out of season.

FASHION STORMS: STAY WARM AND STYLISH IN THE NASTIEST OF WEATHER

By now, your wardrobe is stocked with an arsenal of cute clothes, but all it takes is one snowy, windy, rainy day to throw off your groove. This is why it helps to have some very cute, ridiculously warm pieces in your wardrobe to pull from, taking the guesswork out of it all, giving new meaning to the phrase "wintry mix." Remember, layers are your friend, so round up all of your accessories—scarves, gloves, hats, tights, socks and coats—and do an assessment. If anything looks shabby, ditch it and start over with some quality pieces that really are warm (Hint: Forgo the acrylic scarves for cashmere—it's worth the extra money.)

Layering up can be fun. Whenever it rains or snows, we reach for some of our favorite pieces, like our long wool coat in a punchy color, a floppy wool hat (the better for keeping the flurries out of your face, and it's so chic), a waterproof flannel-lined trench, a cable-knit infinity scarf and cashmere-lined leather gloves. We recommend pillaging end-of-season sales to find these great staples, so you never have to pay full price during the peak of winter.

Now that you've mastered your outerwear, grab a pair of boots you love. Tall boots are the best for really chilly days, as they add another layer of armor against the elements, but ankle boots with chunky socks work well, too. Fleece-lined tights are one of the best-kept secrets ever—they're thin but super warm, so you don't have to eschew wearing a dress just because it's cold outside. Try mixing up your basics: Simple black turtlenecks look cool with colorful pencil skirts and long earrings or wear them under sequin tanks and tucked into black trousers for dressy evenings out. A chunky cardigan can look cool with an oversize statement necklace in jewel-tone colors. Maxi dresses and skirts with boots will keep you warm, but we wouldn't recommend them for snowy days for obvious reasons.

You don't have to sacrifice style just because it's crappy outside. Our biggest piece of advice is to inject some color into your look—even if it's just a printed silk scarf—because all-black-and-gray can be depressing on gray days. It's amazing how a pop of yellow or neon can improve your mood. And don't forget a sweep of bronzer across your face or a colorful lipstick. It makes a world of difference.

WINTER STYLE CONUNDRUMS: WHAT TO WEAR . . .

How to deal with the annoying little fashion problems that creep up during winter, and stay chic all the way through.

WHEN THE INVITE CALLS FOR FESTIVE ATTIRE

The Evites and paper invitations are starting to flow in, and they're calling for "festive attire." No need to be daunted: This means you have carte blanche to pull the most fun pieces out of your closet. Got a sequin dress or a pair of insanely high heels that never see the light of day? This is (finally) their chance to shine.

EASY AS
1, 2, 3

1. Sequin jacket **+** drapey cocktail dress **+** satin platform pumps

2. Embellished sweater dress **+** fleece tights **+** high-heel boots

3. Satin jumpsuit or tuxedo trousers **+** chandelier earrings **+** faux fur wrap

The holidays are all about having fun—opulence, a jovial spirit and, of course, excess. This is the one time of year you can truly get away with wearing— and eating!—anything. After all, the décor is all about tinsel, confetti and sparkly lights, meaning rich fabrics in clothing, like brocade, cashmere or crushed velvet are at home here. They're luxurious fabrics that stand the test of time. If you're feeling like a Grinch, don't forget about the photos: Your ensemble will live on in Facebook or on mantels for years to come, so put some thought into it or you'll be haunted by that uninspired ensemble of Christmas past for years to come.

Remember, no matter how the party turns out, dressing is more than half the fun. If you look great, you'll have a much better time, guaranteed. A great outfit can have a domino effect: When you look good, you feel good and you pass the cheer along. What's more festive than *that*?

TO A HOLIDAY PARTY

If you're anything like us, you'll be eating and drinking to excess at these parties—sorry, diet! So unless you have a super-speedy metabolism, give yourself a little room in your dress. How can you enjoy all the traditional treats that make cocktail parties worthwhile when you can't get past the rolls on your mini-dress? Plus, need we point out that you're more likely to have fun and relax if you can breathe?

This is where A-line dresses come in. Choose one with a fitted waist and a drapey full skirt, or tuck a shimmery top into a brocade skirt. Jackets and oversized embellished cardigans fit in well here, too. Top off the outfit with a sparkly cocktail ring and a pair of jeweled ballet flats or your favorite party shoes with a heel. After a few glasses of eggnog, it can be trickier to maneuver your way home, so make sure you can walk in them!

If you're into pants, go for a wide-leg pair in camel. They look chic with nearly every color (especially red) and they're extremely classic. Or take it up a notch with a silk pair that's fitted at the waist but tapers outward. Pair them with a blouse (not too voluminous if you're the hostess—kitchen disasters and a trip to the emergency room might make a good story, not a good party). Kick it up with an extravagant statement necklace or a silk scarf tied at the neck. A pair of sturdy but chic heels will work well here—you'll look slimmer, too. In general, tuxedo-inspired party pieces don't have to be super-expensive—there are only a few hours of daylight this time of year, so no one will be inspecting whether your pailettes or fur are real or faux. After all, the less you spend on holiday extras, the more you have left for those presents!

EASY AS
1, 2, 3

1. White button-down blouse **+** camel wide-leg pants **+** colorful heels
2. Little black dress **+** faux fur bolero jacket **+** layered necklaces or bangles
3. A-line skirt **+** sequin sweater **+** booties

Survive Inclement Weather during Formal-Event Season

It's such a cruel irony that the parties that allow us to break out the sequins and strappy sandals fall in the dead of winter when there's bound to be a snowstorm to ruin your ensemble. There's no point wearing a gorgeous dress if it ends up hidden under a dreary coat. While we can't change the weather, one thing we suggest making the investment in is a good formal coat. Look for a long coat in velvet, satin or cashmere with some type of fancy detail, be it sequins or braiding. You may not wear it every day, but you'll have the coat at the ready for years. Showing up at the party looking glamorous rather than in your day-to-day puffy coat will help you stand out from the crowd.

Dresses Every Woman Should Have in Her Party Arsenal

1. A little black dress: You can always make it more fun with a cropped fur jacket, a cocktail ring and an embellished clutch or shoes.

2. An A-line shift dress that hits at the knee with sleeves in a bright color—it flatters every single shape.

3. A printed wrap dress in a slinky material, like silk or jersey.

4. A one-shoulder dress: Cleavage can make you look cheap—instead, try showing another, less obvious asset: your gorgeous shoulders.

5. A long gown: If you're attending a black-tie gala or cocktail party, a one-shoulder version will stand out among the millions of strapless dresses out there. In order not to look like you're wearing a paper bag, though, you need to define your waist. Look for styles with a built-in cinch and/or a ruffle across the shoulder. Bonus: You don't need a lot of jewelry—a simple cocktail ring will suffice, along with a chic clutch.

6. A tailored sheath: This is a power look for sure, bringing a hint of sexiness to a dress normally reserved for business meetings. We love this look at work functions, like office holiday parties, because it's elegant and sophisticated and you don't have to do much to accentuate it at all. A pair of earrings will do, and a great pair of heels you love.

7. A cocktail-length dresses: In order not to look like you're going to a toga party, steer clear of white—any other color works. Look for details, like satin or embellishments, to make the look appropriate for evening. A big bow or ruffle is festive and chic.

A Note on Color

If you're not into embellishments, unique color combinations are just as festive. Satin jewel tones are perfect for the holidays—sapphire blues, emerald greens, plum purples, saffron yellows and ruby reds are all gorgeous and can be mixed. Resist any urge to mix red and green, however, unless you are one of Santa's elves. Experiment with mixing unexpected colors instead, like a royal blue dress with red heels. If you typically go for black, you'll probably feel most comfortable in the next best colorful thing: Deep, rich navys and purples will be your go-to hues. If you need inspiration, head over to Kate Spade, who is the master of mixing colors in a chic way, or Diane von Furstenberg, who does it with prints.

TO BEAT THE MIDWINTER (FASHION) SLUMP

By the time February and March hit, the clothes you bought back in December are feeling a little drab. Here we'll show you how to make everything in your closet look better cinched. These five items you're getting sick of from your closet can be instantly transformed with just one item—that's right, a belt.

EASY AS
1, 2, 3

1. Neutral sheath dress + neon or metallic belt + colorful heels
2. Jewel-toned blouse + A-line skirt + red lipstick
3. Colorful or printed sweater + dark-wash jeans + metallic pumps

Cocktail Dress

Take an embellished metallic belt and cinch your natural waist to give an edgy look to your dressiest cocktail dress or evening gown. It adds new life and makes it look a bit more fashion-forward, too. Perfect for the umpteenth cocktail party you get invited to this year when you don't have time (or patience or extra cash) to buy a new dress.

Winter Coat

Add new life to your coat midwinter by adding your coolest belt to it. Try your exotic skin belts (faux is fine, too) for an updated look. Take it even further by pulling out one of your fall coats—you know, the ones with short sleeves or three-quarter-length sleeves—and layering with a turtleneck and elbow-length gloves for a dramatic look ripped straight from the runway.

Oversized Cardigan or Sweater

Take that shapeless sweater and add a colorful, jewel-toned, neon or beaded belt for polish. It's your perfect casual Friday look with jeans and a pair of booties.

Shift Dress

Reinvent the standard shift dress by adding a neutral, medium-width belt. Also try layering with a ribbed turtleneck or faux fur vest over it and tights and pumps under it for an easy, sophisticated look.

Layers at their best—make all of the stuff in your wardrobe work a little.

Flowy Blouse

Take the jewel-toned blouse you typically wear with jeans, add a wide belt, and pair it, untucked, over a voluminous A-line skirt. This is a good stand-in for cocktail parties, too, in a pinch.

WHEN YOUR OFFICE IS SWELTERING!

You made it through the morning snowfall and trudged all the way to work—by foot, by bus or by car—you walk into the office and you're suddenly sweating. The layers you piled on are suffocating you—and now you're supposed to be productive?! Be prepared—just as each office's management style varies, so do the heating levels. If your office tends to be overheated, dress accordingly. Baby, it's all about layers.

If you're wearing a pencil skirt and cardigan, consider wearing a jersey or a silk tee so you can take your outer layer off without feeling self-conscious about baring too much skin. Buy cap-sleeved dresses you can top off with cardigans and, if you favor pants, make sure you don't just wear a heavy sweater or wool blazer—put something light and airy underneath it. If your office tends to be freezing, keep a cashmere sweater in your file cabinet or under your desk to

WEAR THE PANTS

Maybe your legs aren't your best asset, or it's simply too cold to face the elements in a flimsy pair of tights—try tuxedo-inspired pieces instead. Black and white are your best bet and keep you looking classic. In order to avoid being mistaken for the waiter, try a tailored-cut suit rather than a boxy one. Wear your hair flowy, not tied back, to keep it sexy, not severe, and business-like.

EASY AS
1, 2, 3

1. Jersey tee + cardigan + pencil skirt

2. Shift dress + layered necklaces or bangles + blazer

3. Short-sleeved cardigan + trousers + silk tank

throw on. Work can be hectic enough—the last thing you need is to be sweating (or shivering) through the day.

FOR A DAY OF WINTER SPORTS

Few sports are quite as chic as a day on the slopes—hello, ski bunny! Here's how to enjoy your favorite winter activities and still look stylish.

The key is not to bundle up completely—if you end up sweating profusely, your wet clothes will actually make you cold. Your first layer should be long under-wear made of a wicking material—Smart Wool is one of our favorites because it keeps you warm while absorbing any moisture.

Next, layer with a wind- and waterproof jacket and pants. Many companies make feminine ver-sions that are tailored to women's bodies, so you don't have to feel like a big marshmallow when you're out on the slopes. We think sleek black, gray, camel or brown always look smart. Pack some hand warm-ers to put into your waterproof gloves and an extra pair of socks in case yours get too wet after an entire day. It can make all the difference.

If you're going ice skating, throw on some wicking leggings, a lightweight sweater and a scarf. If you're on an ice skating date, we love the sporty but cute look of a striped sweater dress or a jersey dress, fleece tights, a long scarf and a matching beret-style cashmere hat. Don't forget your gloves—it's chilly in the rink. Pack an extra pair of socks for afterwards so you don't have to walk home in sopping wet ones.

EASY AS
1, 2, 3

1. Sweater dress **+** leather jacket **+** fleece tights

2. Oversized knit cardigan **+** wicking leggings **+** cashmere scarf

3. Plaid turtleneck **+** jersey dress **+** knit hat

CHAPTER 4

Look *Très Chic* All Spring

t's the time of year every guy waits anxiously for: when all of those layers of knits, tights and wool coats are shed for lighter, sheerer fabrics and, of course, skin. For women, though, this is a more complicated time: Spring is unpredictable and filled with lots of fashion storms (as well as many *actual* rainstorms)—but your wardrobe shouldn't be. With just a few tweaks—and keeping that good old Girl Scout motto "Always be Prepared" in mind—you'll be ready to take on the coming months. We promise: Whether March goes in like a lion or out like a lamb, you'll always look hot.

THE STRATEGY: WHAT YOU NEED FOR SPRING

This season is all about transition—the moon is in transit, the earth is tilted, and crops, er, we mean, trends, are starting to take hold and grow in full force. You can finally have a little fun with your clothes without worrying too much about the elements. Don't pack away your winter clothes too quickly—you're going to want to keep some pieces out and ready to grab for days when you need more coverage. Spring is a tease, so don't let her catch you off guard. Your spring clothes should have more pops of color, show more skin and, of course, be functional. From the first day without tights (one to celebrate!) to flash floods and spring break jaunts, here's a no-fail list to get you through unscathed:

YOUR SPRING HIT LIST:

☐ A waterproof trench coat with pockets (and removable liner)

☐ A medium-sized umbrella

☐ Stylish waterproof rain boots

☐ A printed dress

☐ Jersey T-shirts

☐ A great pair of jeans that fit you well

☐ A pair of aviator sunglasses or other frames you love

☐ A colorful pencil skirt

☐ A short-sleeved sheath dress

☐ A pair of short boots or moccasins in a light color like tan, metallic, ivory or gray

☐ A pair of ballet flats in a neutral color, like black, metallic or brown

☐ A cool clutch

☐ Some colorful jewelry

☐ A lightweight printed floral scarf

☐ Rain boots that don't look like rain boots

☐ Cotton pants

☐ Shapewear

☐ Canvas sneakers (we love Tretorn or Bensimon)

☐ A cardigan or two for layering (and stuffing in your bag for emergencies)

☐ A leather jacket

☐ A cropped cotton jacket

☐ A colorful belt to freshen up your dark dresses

WHAT'S ON SALE NOW

Spring and summer clothes typically have some overlap, so in May you can frequently pick up light-weight dresses at a discount that will work for the rest of the summer. Also, look for spring accessories like handbags and shoes to start getting marked down in April and a serious cut in May.

TECH EFFECT

If you're going to pack your winter clothes into hibernation for the spring, as we do at the first sign of spring, do yourself a favor and first visit almanac.com/content/frost-chart-united-states to see when the last frost is in your region. Those lucky enough to live in Las Vegas can pack away cold-weather gear in early February, whereas those in Denver had better keep some woolens around until the end of April.

TRENCH CONNECTION

Buy a trench coat that's waterproof (rather than cotton) so you don't get drenched. Get one great trench instead of buying a new one every year. The small investment now will save you lots of time (and closet space) later.

HOW TO ORGANIZE YOUR CLOSET: TIME TO WEED

At this point, wearing the puffy coat or turtleneck again is enough to send anyone over the edge. Say goodbye to all those heavy winter pieces you loathe by now and start pruning to make way for warm-weather items. Keep a cashmere scarf around where you can see it and your rain boots—you never know when you'll need them. This shouldn't be a heavy clean-out—for transitional weather, you're going to want to keep those chunky knit cardigans to layer with your more lightweight springy dresses for a little while. But, ultimately, it'll make your life easier come summer if you've already begun sorting. Hang up all those fun and flirty dresses you've got for summer next to cardigans and blazers you'll wear with them. Try on last year's wide-leg khakis—do they need to be hemmed? Can your wedges from last year be salvaged or do you need a new go-to pair? For work, we like to keep our office-appropriate clothes all together in our closets to eliminate scrambling in the morning. Make your cold-weather accessories easy to reach by storing your hats, scarves, gloves and umbrella in a basket or a bin within reach, or by hanging them nearby. As for shoes, keep your boots together—same goes for pumps, flats and slippers.

Is a Burberry Trench Worth Nearly a Grand?

Now that spring is here, the annoying weather changes are enough to drive everyone mad. And since winter coats are too warm and rain parkas are, well, too ugly, it's time to invest in a classic spring trend: the trench coat. Now we're not just talking about any old trench coat. We are dying for a timeless, iconic Burberry trench (approximately $995). It's a splurge, but after crunching some numbers, it could be cheaper than your morning latte.

With a price tag like this, you're going to want to wear this coat to its maximum potential. We're talking every spring and fall for at least the next handful of years. If you alternate between this coat and another for the next five years—approximately 465 rainstorms—this Burberry coat averages out to cost $2.14 per wear:

> **$995 divided by 465 stylish rainstorms = $2.14/wear**

And anytime we can rock that traditional Burberry check for less than $5 is A-okay with us.

FASHION FLASHBACK . . . BURBERRY

- - - - - - - - - - - - -

Burberry created the iconic "trench coat" when the British war office commissioned the company to create a new officer's coat for wartime in 1914. After the war, civilians began to buy the coat, and today, it's synonymous with effortless chic. Their now-famous trenches, with signature check in pastel, red and black (created in the 1920s) is shorthand for classic, functional and gorgeous. You'll always look pulled together— even when you don't feel like it—whether you're headed to walk the dog or into a job interview. Just don't misplace it!

- - - - - - - - - - -

Burberry

Theory

Calvin Klein

Topshop

Gap

MAKING THE CASE FOR . . .
Wedges

If you've never tried a pair of wedges on, you don't know what you're missing. We've searched high and low for the most comfortable high heels, and wedges win out every single time. The reason? Their platformlike heel makes them easy to walk in—no doing that wobbly dance on the street changing from your flats to heels. Lighten your load by getting a great pair for spring— they make your legs look terrific in all those lightweight dresses you'll be wearing, without sacrificing comfort.

SEASONAL SOS

Ah, spring—nothing feels better than coming out of that long winter hibernation. Which isn't to say the season is free of seasonal style problems: From the extra pounds (or, um, insulation) you packed on over the winter to those April showers, here's how to look chic no matter what the season throws your way.

SOLUTIONS FOR SPRING
FASHION EMERGENCIES

1. Your skin is pasty from hibernating all winter.

SOLUTION: Bring on the bronzer! Sweep it over your face with a good bronzer brush, in spots where the sun would naturally kiss it: in an "M" shape across your face (left cheek, nose, right cheek) and then under your chin. Self-tanner too, should be your friend for those first few days without tights. *Take note:* If you're still going to tanning salons, take a moment and google Snooki. Is that a good enough intervention for you?

2. April showers bring May flowers, ruining all your beloved spring shoes.

SOLUTION: Kate Moss made rain boots cool years ago, so get yourself a stylish pair in black or gray that look like regular boots. That way, you don't have to be embarrassed by your current rubber-duckie pair if you run into a client during off-hours.

Yes, They *Do* Exist

If you have a high instep, meaning you can't pull your boots over the heels of your feet, look for rain boots with a zipper up the back. For extra protection from chilly days, look for our favorite pairs by Loeffler Randall, lined in silk jersey so they're super comfortable.

3. You've put on some pounds since last spring and now nothing fits.

SOLUTION: Don't go on a shopping spree just yet. First, make friends with Spanx. Every year, they come out with new and innovative pieces—now they've even fashioned pencil skirts and tops with built-in shapewear. The technology has come a long way—from leg-shaping skorts to lightweight thongs with built-in tummy tuckers, there's something for every shape.

If you swear you're going to drop the pounds, you can add (or remove) inches from your favorite jeans with Bristol 6's Adjust-A-Button ($18), a simple pin that serves as an extra button for your denim.

4. You dress for spring in the morning, but once the sun goes down, you're left in the cold.

SOLUTION: Trench coats were made for this conundrum. Keep a lightweight cashmere (sometimes called "featherweight") scarf in the pocket so you're ready for inclement weather.

5. You've made the swap from tights to open-toe sandals, but you can barely walk in them now.

SOLUTION: For months, your feet have been inadvertently pampered under all those layers of tights and socks. Band-Aid's Friction Block is a portable solution—just glide the salve onto your feet and it's kind of like wearing invisible tights—no more unsightly blisters. If you're in a bind, a swipe with deodorant will also do the trick.

HOW TO WEAR...
Multiple Prints

There are a few schools of thought about mixing prints. One advocates throwing them together willy-nilly and strutting around, aloof, with a calculated bedhead and expertly smudged dark eyeliner. We will ignore this strategy because, for better or worse, it just doesn't work outside of a fashion editorial.

For us real people with jobs and errands (and without expert stylists), below are three doable tactics that make mixing prints a less formidable task, keeping outfits fresh and fun while maintaining an approachable, sane demeanor.

1 **Stay in the same color family.** Tone down a bold-print floral dress with a striped cardigan that echoes the petals in the dress. This makes the whole thing lighter and less overwhelming.

2 **Choose similar prints in different sizes.** If the circles on your skirt are huge and attention-grabbing, pair them with tiny dots on a ribbed tank. This will keep the pattern from swallowing you up.

3 **Make black and white your friends.** Just about every style is easier to pull off in black and/or white. The combo of huge bright-yellow lemons on a skirt and the thick stripes on a top could look completely cartoonish, but with a black-and-white base, the outfit takes on a whimsical sort of vibe.

FASHION STORMS: PREVENT THE DOWNTRODDEN-WET-DOG LOOK WHEN IT RAINS

While thunderstorms can really be a bummer to your look, a few small solutions can help make rainy days a little more chic. Your life will be filled with the unexpected—inconvenient meetings, rescheduled dinners, and un-welcome, out-of-nowhere downpours. So here's how to be prepared, in style, so you can keep it together even when it's pouring buckets of freezing rain.

With these essentials, you'll always look dry and ready for anything—not downtrodden and drenched:

✦ **A chic pair of rain boots:** The key to looking cool in rain boots is to get a pair that resemble regular boots, but are made of waterproof material so you'll look cute and stay dry, even if you have appointments all over town. When it's cold, we love to wear them with thick fleece tights and wooly dresses.

Goodbye, Rubber Ducky

Don't succumb to the five-year-old, rubber-ducky, rainy-day look. If you're over the age of 11, you shouldn't be wearing chunky, cumbersome rain boots with childlike details on them. If you've got 'em, toss 'em now. Everyone makes mistakes. We'll forgive you, but your boss might not be able to take you as seriously in your next staff meeting if she catches a glimpse of them. Don't take the risk.

✦ **A golf umbrella:** Cheap umbrellas are bound to break—get one good umbrella that's wide enough to cover your upper body and strong enough to weather the biting winds that are likely to accompany the storm. There's nothing worse than being blown away like Mary Poppins and showing up at your destination looking like a wet dog with a broken umbrella. (We've seen it happen.)

✦ **An ultralight umbrella:** Chance of showers? Be prepared with a small, or medium-sized collapsible umbrella, just in case. Totes is known for their super, small, ultralight versions we actually keep in our handbags so we're never caught off guard in a rainstorm.

✦ **A waterproof trench:** Michael Kors, Calvin Klein and DKNY make feminine trench coats at reasonable prices that are also waterproof (see page 90 for more on this), so you don't have to sacrifice style just because it's coming down outside. If there's a detachable hood, even better, just in case, because flash storms are just that—unpredictable.

✦ **Shoe Slickers:** One moment it's sunny, the next, your shoes are ruined by rain. Grab a pair of Shoe Slickers ($4.99 at shoeslickers.com), which are like nylon ponchos for your shoes. They fit over most two- to five-inch heels so you can protect your Louboutins from inevitable water damage. They're lightweight enough, and come with a handy Ziplock baggie, so you can keep them in your purse.

As for your outfit, dresses or skirts are the way to go. You don't want to be walking around with sopping wet hems, so pants are out. If it's cold, tights are the solution—they dry fast so if you do happen to get splashed, you won't be wet all day. Guaranteed, you'll feel so good about yourself, you might even be tempted to jump in a few puddles on the way home.

MAKING THE CASE FOR . . .
Wearing One Color at Once

The monochromatic look is always chic. Try it in a modern way by wearing one bright color, head to toe. This is a great idea if you find that you've been collecting coral-colored things without even realizing it. Wear a silk top, a pair of trousers and a cardigan all in the same color family.

**GO-TO BRANDS
FOR RAIN BOOTS**
- - - - - - - - - - - -

Loeffler Randall

Jeffrey Campbell

Aquatalia

La Canadienne

Hunter

London Fog

SPRING STYLE CONUNDRUMS:
WHAT TO WEAR . . .

April showers bring May flowers . . . and fashion quandaries. Here's the scoop on what to wear to all those tricky spring events.

WHEN FINALLY DINING ALFRESCO

After a long, treacherous winter spent inside with the heat on, it's such a welcome treat to sit at a table in the open air at the first hint of spring. It's no wonder restaurants with outdoor real estate are always the hardest to get into the moment it gets warm outside. Dress with a little panache and maybe you'll get seated a little faster. Just saying.

Brunch Sidewalk-Side

There are few occasions we love more than brunch: It's the perfect excuse to eat Eggs Benedict with alcohol, which, in our minds, is one of the most heavenly combinations. Just as you're allowed to fill your plate like a crazy person, you've also got permission to dress with a little spice to match that Bloody Mary with extra horseradish. Since you'll be sitting in one place, you're more susceptible to getting cold, should gusts of wind or clouds encroach on your breakfast buzz.

This is the time to break out your fun floral maxi-dress that's been mocking you since late summer. Bring a cardigan or cropped jacket, though, because spring afternoons are fickle. You'll need a little room around your waistline later anyway. If your crowd is more casual, throw on a pair of boyfriend jeans with a fitted jersey tee, a blazer or anorak, or a silk or cotton scarf and a pair of moccasins. Bring along an enormous pair of sunglasses. After all, the only thing that should be bloodshot at brunch is your drink.

Romantic Rooftop Dinner

You snagged a reservation to that restaurant with a ridiculous view—and the dress code is just as hard to pin down. Here are some no-fail ideas that will keep you comfortable.

EASYAS
1, 2, 3

1. Maxi dress + chunky wool cardigan + belt
2. Blazer + scarf + boyfriend jeans
3. Denim jacket + boatneck sweater + black ponté pants

EASY AS
1, 2, 3

1. Drapey cocktail dress + leather jacket + strappy heels
2. Silk safari top + colorful pumps + cropped pants
3. Cape + leather skirt + lightweight V-neck

If you're sick of your winter coat, but it's still a little chilly outside, try throwing a cape over your ensemble. It makes eating and reaching across the table for a bite of your date's dish that much easier. Underneath, try a drapey dress in a jewel-toned color (they make everyone look skinny), a pair of pumps or, if it's unseasonably warm, strappy sandals (get a pedicure!) and a leather jacket to show off your cool side and keep you warm when it starts to get chilly.

Picnic in the Park

We love the idea of walking through the park in a pair of wide-leg pants, a button-down under a punchy cardigan with a skinny leather belt and a cute hat. If you're not so into movie moments (this one's a little *Annie Hall*), consider wearing a pair of skinny jeans with your favorite flats, whether they're car shoes or ballet style, together with a trench coat and a thin striped sweater layered over a tank top with a great structured handbag

EASY AS
1, 2, 3

1. Short- or long-sleeved sundress + tights + desert boots

2. Cardigan + tank + skinny jeans

3. Cardigan + printed top + wide-leg trousers

or satchel to fit an impromptu picnic—a baguette and a thermos of wine, of course. Dress in layers, since the sun can come in and out. We love the classic T-shirt and jeans with ballet flats and a lightweight scarf or cardigan, too.

WHILE ROOTING FOR THE HOME TEAM

The weather's fine, school's out and suddenly everyone you know seems to have tickets to a game. Not sure what to wear to root for the home team? We've figured it out for you.

Baseball Games

What should you wear when you have to go to your nephew's T-ball game, or your boyfriend just can't give up those Yankees tickets? We say go with a cute, yet comfortable outfit for the occasion—and don't worry, we're not suggesting you dress like Victoria Beckham, who loves to wear six-inch platform heels to her hubby's soccer matches.

Oversized sunglasses are the essential starting point of any summer outfit—especially for daytime, outdoor events like a sports game. Avoid the back and cleavage sweat that comes with the territory, especially on sunny days, by opting for a breezy, loose-fitting dress. Go for something cotton or even with a linen blend, so it breathes. You don't have to give up being girly just for the sake of the sport.

But forget heels—they'll get stuck in the grass, and they aren't conducive to climbing up bleachers or waiting in line for that mandatory ballpark hot dog. Instead, go for equally chic flat leather sandals, cool sneakers or espadrilles.

Don't skip the facial coverage, especially on hot, sunny days. A straw fedora is perfect—the straw color is versatile and goes with pretty much everything.

If you'd prefer the jeans and tee look, you really can't go wrong with a V-neck. It's universally flattering. Go with stretch, cropped jeans—white is nice. The laid-back style still looks put together. For a comfortable yet sporty look, we love Bensimon shoes, the French flat sneakers that style icons Brigitte Bardot and Jane Birkin made famous in the '60s.

Horse Races

Horse racing is a fun way to get outdoors and even win a few bucks if you're feeling lucky. On opening days at major tracks like the Preakness, the Belmont Stakes and the Kentucky Derby, the crowd is festive and loud, so go ahead and wear a fun sundress with a splashy print, a pair of strappy sandals, and bring along a jacket just in case it gets cold. Throw on a lightweight scarf and a cross-body bag to keep the cash you win close to you. A seersucker blazer always looks good with a mint julep and will keep you warm when the sun starts to set.

EASY AS
1, 2, 3

1. Skinny white jeans + striped tee + ballet flats
2. V-neck tee + madras shorts + casual flat sneakers, like Tretorns
3. Linen dress + straw fedora + flat sandals

If you're heading to the Kentucky Derby (or even a Kentucky Derby party, no matter where you live), it's all about the hat. You don't have to get one custom-made, like the Southern belles, just make sure it's huge—and fabulous. If you're even a little bit embarrassed by it, it's not your hat. Put it back, girl: The one you choose should feel right and complement your style or you'll just feel like a phony, and you won't have fun. Make sure it's big and floppy to give you that Audrey Hepburn look that's so timeless. It matters less what you're wearing—literally, everyone will be looking at your hat (especially if it's a great one), but don't go too casual. The South is a little more strict about dress codes, adhering to myths like "no white before Memorial Day" and since the Derby falls in early May, we'd stick with a print or a bright color. Sip that julep and don't forget to smile, y'all!

If you're going to a horse race on other, not-so-special days, leave the hat at home. It's a million times more casual on regular weekend days, so dress for the weather and make sure your footwear is comfortable. You'll be trekking from your seat to go look at the horses before each race, not to mention the bet counter to place your bets. Stick with flats. These days will be filled with regulars, who are way more focused on the races—and their winnings—than on your outfit.

EASY AS
1, 2, 3

1. Floppy straw hat **+** sundress **+** wedges
2. Oversized hat **+** maxi-dress **+** flat sandals
3. Boatneck long-sleeved tee **+** skinny jeans **+** scarf

Golf Outings

Whether you're going to Augusta National or you're riding along in the cart during a fun tournament, keep it low-key. Golf is the quietest game around, and its players view it as a sacred act. Same goes for attire: It's the least showy, most understated sport, fashion-wise, but the underlying theme is crisp and classic sportswear. Wear a polo shirt and a pair of bermuda shorts and a pair of soft flats (driving shoes work). Don't offend the old geezer members by wearing super-short shorts, and don't even *try* to wear a pair of heels—they'll poke holes in that prize-winning golf course. For your best-case scenario, check the website of

EASY AS
1, 2, 3

1. Polo shirt +
   bermuda shorts
   + driving shoes
2. Gingham top +
   white, cropped
   cotton pants
   + scarf
3. Button-down
   tee + cropped
   khaki trousers +
   Bensimon sneakers

the country club or even consider calling ahead to inquire before going: Some clubs have no-shorts rules and don't allow sleeveless shirts at all. Bring along a straw hat or a visor if you prefer—sunglasses, too, will keep you looking chic and sporty.

Tennis Matches

The key is to blend in without looking like you're about to take on Serena Williams. Wear a button-down shirt, a lightweight cardigan, cotton pants (in khaki or white, of course) with a skinny belt and a pair of comfortable shoes, whether they're Tod's or TOMS, you'll be happy later on when you're not hobbling around like a Williams sister just kicked your butt. Don't forget your sunglasses and a straw hat. Not too big, though—your seatmates may complain. If it's hot, wear a lightweight dress with pockets and comfortable shoes. Spring breezes may blow, but the sun can be strong in the stands.

EASY AS
1, 2, 3

1. Sundress **+** cardigan **+** hat

2. Printed blouse **+** jeans **+** cropped jacket

3. Button-down top **+** shorts **+** Bensimon sneakers

HOW TO WEAR . . .
a Flowy, Boho Waist, without Looking Pregnant

Dresses and tops with empire waists—raised waistlines that fall right below the bust—can be fantastic for hiding a thicker middle or showing off a stunning décolletage. Unfortunately, wearing a poorly fitting empire (pronounced ahm-PEER) can also put your friends and coworkers on unnecessary bump watch. To avoid looking preggers while wearing one of the summer's most comfortable and flattering trends, follow a few simple shopping guidelines:

1 **Look for fabrics like ultracomfortable jersey or silk.** Loose, flowy fabrics drape better and skim the body in all the right spots without clinging or adding extra weight under the bust, so they won't inspire an 'Is-she-or-isn't-she' debate.

2 **Make sure the tightest part of the top cinches just below your bustline, where your rib cage is the smallest.** A too-high waist can make your breasts look squished, and a too-low waist can give the illusion of droopiness in all the wrong places.

3 **Balance is key when it comes to dresses.** A hemline that falls midknee to two inches below your knee shows just the right amount of leg, so you avoid looking top-heavy or lost in a sea of billowy fabric.

{ CHAPTER 5 }

Sizzle with Summer Style

Finally, it's summer—the time we've been waiting for all year long. We get to wear whatever we want, as long as it's lightweight—from flowing fabrics and cool prints to punchy colors and open-toe shoes. Once you've got your wardrobe in order, all you need is a pedicure.

THE STRATEGY: WHAT YOU NEED FOR SUMMER

This season is all about fun and effortlessly cool outfits—it's hot outside and, baby, there are plenty of picnics, day trips, BBQs and impromptu parties to attend, not including lots of opportunities to don a new swimsuit. All your hard wardrobe work for spring will come in handy—many of your transition-weather pieces will still work seamlessly for summer. And don't forget to take a breather from real life, too: Everyone needs a vacation, even if you're staying in town. Here in New York, we call it a "stay-cation," where you can spend some time at the pool, beach or nearby park (and look good doing it). Your summer clothes should be colorful, airy and breathable—from those scorching days of humidity to jaunts to the beach or country, here's your go-to list to see you through those long summer days without even thinking about it.

YOUR SUMMER HIT LIST

- ☐ Three tank tops, or more, depending on how much you layer
- ☐ Five T-shirts
- ☐ A striped shirt
- ☐ An Oxford shirt
- ☐ A great pair of sunglasses
- ☐ A statement necklace
- ☐ A straw clutch
- ☐ A jersey dress
- ☐ A pair of white jeans
- ☐ A colorful bikini
- ☐ A black swimsuit—one- or two-piece; your call
- ☐ A pair of canvas sneakers
- ☐ A canvas tote
- ☐ A cashmere/silk-blend shawl
- ☐ A swim cover-up
- ☐ A pair of flat sandals
- ☐ A little white dress(es)
- ☐ Luggage
- ☐ A maxi-dress or skirt
- ☐ A pair of nude-colored underwear
- ☐ A one-piece swimsuit
- ☐ A safari jacket
- ☐ A white blazer
- ☐ A pair of shorts (a flattering pair, of course!)

- [ ] Spanx
- [ ] A straw hat
- [ ] A tropical-weight wool sheath dress
- [ ] A pair of wedge espadrilles
- [ ] A set of bangles, to layer

WHAT'S ON SALE NOW

Markdowns start in mid-July, so that's when you should buy the hot summer fashion trends you've been coveting. July is a good time to pick up a new swimsuit, too, so plan your vacation for later in the summer so you don't go broke on such a minimal amount of fabric. Save the money for the piña coladas instead. In mid-August, the selection will be more limited, but you'll score the serious deals. August is a great time to pick up accessories like sunglasses and hats—just make sure you buy timeless styles so you won't look like a freak wearing a pair of outdated sunglasses next year when the trend is so over. The key is to check back often to monitor the stock and discounts. You'll frequently find yourself in a bit of a dilemma because the inventory could be low, but if you wait the price may drop even further.

FASHION
FLASHBACK . . .
RAY-BAN AVIATORS

You know how maga-
zines always tell you
to determine your
face shape in order
to figure out what
sunglasses to wear?
Forget it—aviators
work for every single
face shape. Ray-Ban
Aviators (first de-
veloped for hot-air
balloon adventurers
in 1936) were adopted
by the U.S. Air Force
for their ability to
protect soldiers from
the sun. In World War
II, General Doug-
las McArthur was
photographed in a
pair, and they've been
an American staple
since. The "aviator"
design has been in

HOW TO WEAR . . .
Black Shoes in the Summer

Black shoes during the summer sounds like an
oxymoron, doesn't it? Yet black shoes, particularly heels, can work well with summer outfits,
especially if you're off to a less-than-casual
dinner party or your office doesn't observe any
sort of warm-weather-induced lax dress code.

In fact, in these cases, a pair of black heels can
help keep the rest of your summer clothes looking
crisp and pulled together.

To begin, keep the shoe simple, with a high heel
that's not too chunky and thus won't overwhelm
your look. It's also a good idea to wear a shoe
that's relatively hardware-free (those zippers and
other embellishments can wait until fall).

A great way to wear black heels is with a punchy
skirt and tank, which can help temper the look.
They also come in handy when you're mixing
prints (see page 93), as they provide a solid
anchor for all of those busy fabrics.

HOW TO ORGANIZE YOUR CLOSET FOR HEAT WAVES

There is a whole slew of great trends you can finally wear outside—with practically nothing to worry about, except heat waves. You know how all the best fruit is in season during summer? It's the same with trends—now you just have to choose which flatter your body and you're set. Stash your closed-toe booties, boots, and tights and make room for strappy sandals—you'll also need to get yourself a good pedicurist. Keep a pair of flats around (you'll need them!) and your rain boots can stay, too, for spontaneous thunderstorms that are likely to crop up. Keep a few lightweight cardigans or a thin leather, linen or denim jacket within reach for chilly late nights—as the days get longer, you'll stay out later, and a chill is bound to come through. Move the flirty summer dresses to the forefront, along with a blazer for work—the air-conditioning will be unbearable some days, and you don't want to be shivering when you should be giving a flawless presentation. Try on last year's tunics, shorts, swimsuit and whatever else you've been hiding away. If it doesn't fit or looks too worn, let it go.

style ever since, now seen on famous faces everywhere from *Top Gun* to today's off-duty fashion models and A-listers. The key is to go neutral—mirrored lenses or shiny frames (not to mention rhinestones) negate the understated cool factor.

TAKE FLIGHT: FIVE GO-TO BRANDS FOR AVIATORS

- - - - - - - - - - - - -

MICHAEL Michael Kors

Marc by Marc Jacobs

Ralph Lauren

A.J. Morgan

Ray-Ban

- - - - - - - - - -

Unlined white or nude
swimsuits

Boob underhang

Thongs

G-strings

Anything that gives
you a hideous tan line

SWIMSUIT SHOPPING MADE EASY

The best advice we can give you when trying to find your perfect swimsuit is first look in your closet. See a pattern? Is everything black or are all of your favorite shirts paisley prints? That's probably the color you find most flattering on your body, so you'll feel more comfortable in it. If your favorite dress is a red halter or the top you always gravitate to is a strapless navy number, your swimsuit should follow—it's a no-brainer, and the easiest way to find what flatters you.

We suggest trying swimsuits on at a department store, then shopping online later—you'll find the best deals that way. You can thank us later.

Yes, They *Do* Exist

Spanx swimwear is the answer to any woman who dreads the moment when she has to put on a bathing suit. The geniuses behind the successful shapewear brand have infused a new line of one-pieces and bikinis with slimming technology. No more hiding behind that sarong. Get out there!

Body-Con: The Best
Swimsuits for Your Shape

It's every woman's tiniest piece of clothing, but it causes the most trouble—and tears. Here's how to shop for a swimsuit and bypass all the ones that clearly aren't right for you. If only we could employ this trick while dating, we'd save a lot of heartbreak.

THE PITFALLS:

Tankinis tend to ride up, and belly-baring bikinis aren't doing you any favors, either.

THE TRICKS:

One-pieces don't have to be matronly—just make sure you have the right size. Trick the eye with low-cut V-neck tops, halters, ruching or a high-cut leg—all these attributes draw attention away from your middle.

THE PITFALLS:

You need a swimsuit to flatter both your top and your bottom. Steer clear of boy shorts, which will only make you look wider, and don't be afraid to mix and match sizes. (You could be a 4 up top and a 10 on the bottom—swimsuits are not one-size-fits-all.)

THE TRICKS:

Try solids on the bottom and go crazy with prints on the top. This helps to balance out your assets. Or try a black bottom and a solid, lighter color on top. For a longer, leaner look, try high-cut bottoms, but steer clear of the string bikini bottoms, which will only emphasize your thighs.

HOURGLASS SHAPES

THE PITFALLS:

You have the ideal figure for a bikini so the only thing to keep in mind is to make sure you have enough support up top, and that the bottoms don't fall off or ride up.

THE TRICKS:

Try a halter bikini top that will lift and support your bust. If you are blessed in the chest area, look for a suit with thicker straps— you can get the sexy vibe going by choosing a one-piece with a deep V.

RECTANGLE SHAPES

THE PITFALLS:

You have a va-va-voom look in mind, but your lack of womanly curves makes you feel more like a teenage boy, or worse, a SpongeBob SquarePants look-alike.

THE TRICKS:

If you want to go one piece, look for swimsuits that have a form-fitting waist with a dark stripe around your middle. This will give the illusion of curves. Bikini bottoms with ruffles or side ties will help your hips look fuller and offset your lack of a defined waist. To add more *oomph* to your bust, look for tops with patterns and details like studs or chains.

THE PITFALLS:

Many petite swimsuits for small busts are created with tons of synthetic padding—not only is it itchy and uncomfortable, it's also noticeable after you take a dip.

THE TRICKS:

Try underwire. You'll get a lift and some shape, without flattening you out or adding an artificial pad. Don't be afraid of details like ruffles, beading and pleats—they add some va-va-voom to your look by bulking up your bust and creating balance. Be wary of bandeau styles—while they're cute, they can make you look flatter.

THE PITFALLS:

It's hard to find a suit with enough support to feel comfortable on the beach. So many styles are too flimsy or too revealing, leading to sagging and spillage that's not so hot.

THE TRICKS:

Go for cups big enough to hold you in with wider bands to give you the support you need. A tie in the back is better than those clasps that can break or bend. Steer clear of triangle tops, ruffles or high necklines (ahem, uni-boob). For the best support, choose between an underwire or a halter top. Solid, jewel-tone colors tend to be best for this body type.

THE PITFALLS:

Many plus-sized swimsuits have high necks, low-cut legs and large prints that stretch out—not cute.

THE TRICKS:

Try pleated, ruched suits, small graphic prints and tankinis that are solid on bottom and printed on top to trick the eye into seeing a slim line. Stripes can look cool on every body type, as long as they're vertical or angled, not horizontal, which will only make you look wider. Wrap styles, just like the dresses, create a thinner waist—you've got to try it. If you want to wear a bikini, go with thicker straps and make sure you tie the halter correctly to support your bust. Don't even think about trying on those granny suits with the skirts—if we spot you, we're calling you out and staging an intervention.

Five One-Piece Swimsuits That Are Sexy, Not Senior Citizen-Worthy

Bikinis aren't for everyone. Chances are, if you wouldn't wear a crop top, you're probably leaning more toward the one-piece style, which tends to get a bad rap for being a little on the prudish side. We're proving 'em wrong with these go-to styles we love:

1 **Lace-up fronts:** They add some sex appeal to the standard one-piece.

2 **Ruching:** Gathered material hides all your lumps and rolls.

3 **Retro halters:** Thin, '50s-style halters draw the eye up—and evoke an irresistible pinup girl look.

4 **Low-cut V-necks:** Show off some serious skin—it doesn't get hotter than this.

5 **Red:** It's a proven fact that guys think red is the sexiest color on earth. Why do you keep buying all of those black swimsuits again? Give it a whirl, girl.

SEASONAL SOS

From finding a bra to wear with those cute summer tops to breaking out the bikini again, we've got the solution for all your summer dilemmas.

SOLUTIONS FOR SUMMER FASHION EMERGENCIES

1. Your headlights are on, and people are staring.

SOLUTION: Backless, deep V-necks, off-the-shoulder, sheer and mesh—all these shirt styles can make it virtually impossible to find a bra that works. Those in the burlesque industry know them as pasties, but you can get a glitter-free pair to match your skin tone from a variety of brands. We like Bristol's natural-looking Silicone Nippie Skins—they're soft and have a strong adhesive that won't come off even if you're sweaty.

2. Your strapless bra creeps down your torso, making you afraid to move.

SOLUTION: Try Fashion Forms Nu Bra. A self-adhesive bra may sound crazy, but it's useful in myriad ways, especially for strapless styles, deep V-necks or other tricky necklines. They give you gentle support, so you're not completely letting the girls hang low.

3. Your new sandals are totally unkind to your poor feet.

SOLUTION: A little bit of lubrication keeps uncomfortable rubbing from creating more blisters. You can buy a Body Glide Stick—the brand surfers use to fend off wet-suit chafing. It'll stop a hot spot from developing into a blister. If you're in a bind, you can also swipe the spot with some solid deodorant. It won't last as long, but will buy you some time until you can get out of those shoes.

Make your super-high wedge sandals a walk in the park to wear by slipping invisible gel cushions into them like Dr. Scholl's For Her Ball of Foot Cushion or Foot Petal's Tip Toes. These pads provide extra padding for the balls of your feet, which are bearing most of the weight. We've also heard of people getting collagen shots into the balls of their feet so they can withstand hours in heels, but we think this is a bit extreme (although if someone would like to give us a free treatment, we're up for it).

4. Hello, warm weather. Hello, pit stains.

SOLUTION: Prevent underarm sweat marks with Garment Guard Clothing Protectors—just stick the cotton discs on the inside of your top, and throw them out when the day is over. If you do end up with a sweaty shirt, freshen it up with a deodorizer like Febreze or Tide Swash Fresh It Up. Keep a stash at the office, at home and in the car.

5. Fabrics got sheerer and shapes slimmer and now your muffin top is on display.

SOLUTION: The key is shirring. Tops or sheath dresses with shirring will help disguise that little bit of extra flesh. You also want to pay a visit to the shapewear aisle and invest in a layering tank top with compression for the midsection. Spanx and Yummie Tummie both make good options for keeping the flesh from spilling over your waistband.

6. I have no idea what shoes to wear with short dresses, rompers and shorts.

SOLUTION: Try a sexy, bare heel for a grown-up look that looks awesome with all your short dresses. Round toes and Mary Janes are too little-girl. If you're wearing evening shorts or rompers, choose a more substantial style, like a platform to balance out the look.

FASHIONMATH:
What You Should Drop Your Dough on This Season

REVERSIBLE CANVAS TOTE

We're crushing on a new kind of canvas bag that you can wear two ways. If you're an L.L. Bean canvas tote kind of girl, we suggest you upgrade. It can be a tough pill to swallow, but we're eyeing Tory Burch's Reversible Canvas Tote ($195)—it's much more than just a beach bag. It's sturdy and chic enough to wear to work, on the weekends, shopping, etc. Plus, the bag has two great reversible sides—so you're really getting two bags in one. We're huge fans of Tory Burch (and of a great-quality bag), but we had to crunch the numbers before justifying this purchase.

{ **$195 divided by 90 stylish summer and fall days = $2.17/wear** }

In the end, the numbers don't lie: A bag that lasts forever is worth ten that don't. (If you don't agree, just think: Are you still carrying your most expensive handbag purchases? Are the cheapies collecting dust?) Plus, a bag that you will lug everywhere from the office to the airport and beyond should be well-made and good-looking.

FLIP-FLOPS

Flip-flops usually aren't chic, but Bernardo Miami flip-flops (around $89) are, considering they were Jackie O's favorites for exotic vacations. A-listers with classic style, like Reese Witherspoon and Halle Berry, still wear the sandals today. What makes them so special? They're handcrafted with Nappa leather and come in lots of colors (Jackie O owned the sandals in sixteen different shades). They're incredibly comfortable, but dressy enough to wear with a maxi-dress out for drinks, too. Is $89 too much for a pair of flip-flops? Let's do the fashion math:

> **$89 divided by 48 stylish summer days = $1.85/wear**

If you wear these sandals four days out of the week for the entire summer, they cost less than a popsicle from the ice cream man. We would choose these flip-flops over a cheap rubber variety any day.

INVESTMENT BIKINI

The wrong bikini can ruin a day at the beach *and* magnify all your body's flaws. French brand Eres is a 40-year-old company that makes luxury swimwear that's pretty pricey, but it never lets you down. The Eres Swim Show Bandeau Bikini Top ($210) and Eres Swim Jane Bikini Bottom ($120) are made with a fabric that sculpts the body and doesn't require padding or boning, plus the material is dipped in a potion that helps it keep its shape so it always looks good, no matter how many times you wear it. But if you still aren't convinced, check out the fashion math:

{ $330 divided by 160 fun days at the beach = $2.06/wear }

If you wear this bikini to the beach or pool twenty times over the course of eight summers, it's cheaper than a large bottle of water for your beach bag. We understand the allure of $10 bikinis from a bin, but they don't last past one summer. You will wear this bikini over and over for years to come and it will still look good.

FASHION STORMS: HOW TO STAY COOL DURING A HEAT WAVE

We all know those summer days, when it's so unbearably hot and muggy out that your hair frizzes before it even finishes drying and the last thing you want to do is put on clothes. Here's our go-to list of staples for the dog days of summer:

✦ Linen anything (we wish they made linen underwear).

✦ Flattering shorts.

✦ A loose-fitting top (no pit stains here).

1. Printed linen skirt
   + tucked-in tank
   + flat sandals
2. Shirt dress + belt +
   slingback pumps
3. Tee + silk shorts
   + wedges

✦ Shirt dresses—your legs may be sticking together, but at least you'll *look* cool.

✦ Lightweight maxi-dresses.

✦ Flat sandals.

✦ Brightly colored tank dresses.

Body-Con: The Best Dresses to Hide Your Tan Lines

It's that time of year—wedding season is in full swing. And the worst fashion offense a guest can commit (second only to wearing white) is showing up with tan lines blazing. Sure, your best friend's destination wedding in Vieques is the perfect time to get your summer glow on—just make sure your preparty swimsuit shape matches your dress silhouette.

The Culprit: The Tank Swimsuit or the Asymmetrical Swimsuit

The Solution: A sleeveless dress. Don't be that girl in the strapless dress with two white lines outlined on your shoulders or, even worse, one white shoulder and one dark. You want to look put together, not like you just rolled off the beach towel. A sleeveless dress allows you to show off your newly tanned arms without showing where you forgot to apply sunscreen.

The Culprit: The String Bikini

The Solution: A halter dress that follows the lines of the string bikini will allow you to show off a bronzed back without the telltale tie-lines.

The Culprit: The Bandeau Top

The Solution: A strapless dress. Bandeau tops tend to ride high on the chest, so if you wear a V-neck or a backless dress, you risk revealing the white stripe around your torso. Instead, match the edge of the bikini top to a strapless dress that stops at the same point or higher.

We love the look of evening shorts, especially on nights when it's so hot you can't bear even the slightest bit of extra material on your body. Try a nude palette with lots of texture. For example, we love lightweight metallic mini-shorts that are tailored, paired with gray leather pumps and a flowing top, a tucked-in button-down tunic or a cropped jacket. It's all a balancing act at night. Don't do a tank and a pair of shorts and heels—it's far too much skin and you might get mistaken for a streetwalker.

SUMMER STYLE CONUNDRUMS: WHAT TO WEAR . . .

It's summertime, and the fashion is tricky. Here's the scoop on just what to throw on, no matter what's on the agenda for those sizzling summer days and long summer nights.

TO THE OUTDOOR BBQ

Whether it's on a roof, New York City–style, or on a large, open, grassy knoll during July Fourth, with fireworks all around, outdoor BBQs call for a festive sundress and flat, strappy sandals. But, as we always say, *Don't wear white to Chili Fest*, which is shorthand for know your venue. Grab yourself a print or, even better, your favorite red sundress—the better to hide those inevitable blobs of barbecue sauce that somehow find their way onto your favorite dresses. Not only will you be less stressed and more comfortable (none of that legs-sticking-together stuff), but you'll look effortlessly cute, too. Plus, you never know who you might meet: The chances of scoring a date become exponentially higher when the weather is warm—all the cute guys have finally come out of hiding!

EASYAS
1, 2, 3

1. Printed sundress **+** belt **+** sunglasses

2. Safari dress **+** flat sandals **+** hat

3. Romper **+** wrap bracelets **+** flat sandals

TO THE BEACH

Is there anything more fun than taking a break from your laptop and the trappings of your office to flock to a big strip of sand to lie in the sun with friends, reading gossip magazines and dipping in the ocean? Not in our minds. When you're heading to the beach for the day, do yourself a favor and pack light. The long walk in the sand with the sun beating down on you is a million times easier if you leave the cooler and chairs at home and just bring the necessities. Wear a printed tunic and shorts, or a chic printed caftan with your swimsuit

EASYAS
1, 2, 3

1. Bikini + caftan + sunglasses
2. Swimsuit + shorts + flowy blouse
3. Tunic + shorts + hat

underneath, a floppy straw hat and slip-on sandals. Bring along a roomy straw tote or canvas bag, filled with sunscreen, a beach towel and some bottled water. (And don't forget a change of underwear.) Now go have some fun, and take a sun-and-sea-soaked nap for us while you're at it.

TO LOOK CUTE WHILE CAMPING (YES, IT'S POSSIBLE)

When you agree to go camping, you're signing up for what's supposed to be a low-maintenance trip, so it's best to be prepared beforehand and really think about what the weather will be like and what kind of adventures you'll be embarking on before heading out. You're going to have to be practical, so obviously hair dryers and heels are not welcome, sadly. You'll need a windbreaker, in case of rain, and a fleece pullover in a flattering color. Black is always best, and go sleek in a pair of leggings with wicking material. Bring wool socks and a pair of hiking boots or sneakers with support, and a pair of shorts for daytime. When camping, you need to remember, no cotton: It will take forever to dry. You'll need lightweight, easy to pack, warm pieces that are also water-resistant. Have fun, and don't forget the bug spray!

EASY AS
1, 2, 3

1. Parka **+** leggings **+** desert boots

2. Waterproof shorts **+** tee **+** sneakers

3. Windbreaker **+** fleece pullover **+** waterproof pants

1, 2, 3

1. Shift dress + belt + wedges
2. Oxford top + dark denim + necklace
3. Jersey tee + bermuda shorts + cardigan

TO THE COMPANY PICNIC

Ah, the company picnic. An obligatory event that eats up your Saturday and forces you to see quirky coworkers outside their normal habitat in inappropriate and outright dorky attire. But since you have to go, arrive looking casual, conservative and stylish. It's supposed to be a day of fun but you're still technically at work, even if it's held outdoors. Don't bare too much skin or wear your most comfortable, well-worn clothes. Wear a structured, short sleeve, A-line dress with a belt and peep-toe sandals and you'll still look put together. Or for a more casual look that's still pulled together, try a silk, neutral-colored shell tucked into a bright mid-length skirt in a summery color, like yellow or coral, flat sandals, and a long chunky necklace. It's a good mix of structure with personality—and if you have to sit in the grass for pow-wows, you won't be self-conscious about the guy from accounting getting a peek up your dress. If your office is super-casual, wear something you'd wear on casual Friday: A pair of dark jeans or linen trousers and peep-toe flats with a white oxford shirt and a statement necklace will fit the bill. A pair of solid bermuda shorts are another safe option as your boss may force you to participate in a wiffle-ball game or a three-legged race, and that sundress you considered would prove too risky. Wouldn't

want your boss to think you're not a team player!
Wear those Bermuda shorts with a lightweight,
loose-fitting blouse that you can tuck in. Add a
belt to look more pulled together, and slip on some
colorful wedges instead of too-casual flip-flops.

Store your camera in a structured, straw tote—
the better to document for blackmail during the
potato sack race—and don't forget your shades
to hide those inevitable eye rolls.

TO OUTDOOR MUSIC FESTIVALS

Dressing for a concert is solely contingent on what kind of music you're going to see. You'd never wear white to a funeral, right? In the same way, you'd never wear a sundress to the Vans Warped tour or a studded belt to Coachella. In terms of outdoor summer concerts, there are often two types of events.

If you're going to an outdoor concert with more of a festival vibe (like Coachella or Bonnaroo), look for references to the 1960s and '70s—we're talking crochet, cutoffs and flowers galore. We get it: You're not a hemp-wearing Grateful Dead fan, but you can still look boho-chic and comfortable at the outdoor concerts and festivals this summer. Have no fear—there is a stylish way to wear hippie-inspired clothing (thanks for the inspiration, Kate Hudson and Kate Moss).

We're huge fans of the summer maxi-dress—flowy and easier to sway to the music. Whether you look better in halter styles or strapless depends on your bust. If your body gets lost in maxis, try a bright and flowy skirt with a tucked-in tank, a funky necklace and a cross-body bag so you don't lose your purse. If it's during the day, don't forget your coolest pair of sunglasses (consult whatever style Mary-Kate and Ashley are wearing at the moment or go with the never-fail aviator look) and consider a straw fedora in a color so you can be easily spotted in a crowd. A cool, wild print not only fits the venue, but it makes it easier for your friends to see you when you get separated at the mosh pit later. Flat, strappy sandals are a must—you'll likely have to walk far, and it can get muddy. If you must wear heels, wedges are the way to go.

To accessorize, wrap a simple leather strap around your wrist a couple of times. If the show has more of a packed concert vibe (like Ultra or the Vans Warped tour), you might want to stay away from skimpy dresses and open-toed shoes (given your likelihood to be near a mosh pit at any given time). Regardless of the type of music that will be playing, though, always make sure you wear something that's comfortable and something that you don't mind getting dirty—trust us, you won't have properly enjoyed the show if you don't leave with some combination of dust, grass stains and popsicle juice on your clothes.

In terms of an indoor concert, look for something fun—concerts are a great excuse to wear something a little out of the box that you wouldn't wear normally. (And don't be afraid to experiment—unlike at a bar, people are preoccupied with watching the band, not you.) As long as your outfit keeps you cool and lets you dance, feel free to go wild. One tip, however: If it's the type of show that will have black lights overhead (think electronic and house music shows, plus some concerts at smaller venues), avoid wearing black at all costs— the black dress you're wearing will fade away, and every little speck of lint on it will show through, making you look just plain dirty.

MAKING THE CASE FOR . . .
the Little White Dress

Also known as the LWD, the little white dress is just as chic as your trusty old little black dress, but more seasonally appropriate. Forget the myth that white makes everyone look fat. When it's hot outside, it's really the only "color" we want to wear. Try textured versions, embroidery, cut-outs, origami details and even eyelet. For evening, it's white-hot sexy with metallic accessories, and during the day it looks pretty with nude or gray.

{ CHAPTER 6 }

No-Fail Fashion for Fall

This season is all about buckling down from the leisurely pace of summer, and turning over a new leaf, so your wardrobe should reflect the change. It's time to get more serious about your work wardrobe—casual summer Fridays are over, and weekends are all about the layers. You'll spend less time outside and start to prepare your closet for the transition to cold weather. But the good news is that it's still warm enough for outdoor activities, like apple picking, Oktoberfest beer festivals and trick-or-treating. Holidays like Thanksgiving are right around the corner, kicking off a myriad of parties and get-togethers as people spend more time with their families and loved ones.

At this point, take a look at the spring holdovers in your closet: You can try to refashion them with a few tweaks. All those cute, flowy dresses can be paired with cardigans or blazers, booties and tights. You can probably still get away with open-toe leather sandals, too, so if you've got 'em, you can still get some wear out of them until it turns cold. Your fall clothes should be cozy yet breathable—and you should always be prepared for those unpredictable days where the weather changes on a whim and gets a little too hot or too cold. Here's your go-to list to see you through those cool autumn days without a snafu in sight.

THE STRATEGY:
WHAT YOU NEED FOR FALL

Summer is winding down and the days are getting cooler—finally! This is one of the most anticipated, riveting times of the year for the fashion world. It's no coincidence that Mercedes Benz Fashion Week kicks off in September, when all the major designers around the world will show their new wares to the fashion elite: magazine editors, department store buyers and the occasional Real Housewife. It's the fashion set's equivalent of the first day of school. It's so exciting to pick out what you'll be wearing for the rest of the year now that everyone's back from summer vacation and ready to get back to business. Fashion insiders start dreaming about pulling on the layers and accessories again, and the magazines are the fattest of the year. Fall is all about newness—churning over the closet, just as farmers turn their soil for the close of their growing season. Look forward to restocking your closet with new boots, denim, handbags and more that you'll go back to again and again.

YOUR FALL HIT LIST

- [ ] Three to five layering tanks and tees
- [ ] Wool sheath dress
- [ ] Cozy oversized sweater or cardigan to wear over dresses, with jeans, etc.
- [ ] Wool or wool-blend pants—one black, one gray, one camel
- [ ] White button-down shirt
- [ ] At least one pair of tall leather boots (some boot-lovers prefer one in black and one in brown)
- [ ] Booties
- [ ] Cashmere cardigan
- [ ] Printed scarf
- [ ] Suede moccasins or driving shoes
- [ ] Overnight bag
- [ ] Thin socks
- [ ] A combination of gray and black tights
- [ ] Navy, black or gray blazer
- [ ] Leather jacket
- [ ] Great-fitting pairs of jeans (one wide-leg, one skinny, one boot cut, if they're flattering on you)
- [ ] A fabulous leather handbag
- [ ] Camel-colored trousers
- [ ] A skinny belt, to go over cardigans, pants and pencil skirts
- [ ] Shell tanks, in a multitude of colors
- [ ] Blouses for work and evening
- [ ] Plaid top
- [ ] Boatneck sweater
- [ ] Leggings

A long cardigan is a versatile, perennially practical item that has the potential to look great when styled right—think sexy librarian instead of "frump." And what with overzealous office air-conditioning and cool late-summer nights that take you by surprise, a long cardigan is a perfect emergency layer to keep folded up in your bag, desk or car.

Start simple, with a long, lean gray knit. You can accessorize this in almost any direction you choose, though a long pendant will stand out well and help elongate your look. A solid-color long cardigan looks good over a printed dress that's almost the same length. Be sure to go with a dress with a bit of structure, so you're not rocking the drapey-hippie look. A nipped waist will add some nice definition under the sweater.

Last, an edgy handbag, with interesting hardware details, and cute flats will keep the entire look thoroughly modern.

WHAT'S ON SALE NOW

In September and early October, you can pick up some serious deals on end-of-summer fashion. Starting in October, you'll see deals on the ultratrendy fall items that didn't sell out—think peep-toe booties. By November, retailers are gearing up for the head rush of Black Friday. Only now the retailers' desire to outsale each other has made it so some Black Friday sales start way back in October. However, the big week for Black Friday is Thanksgiving week. Most of the deals are on gifts and electronics, but you will see some retailers slashing prices storewide, so it's worth being on their email lists to get a heads-up about what they've got planned.

FASHION FLASHBACK . . . FRYE BOOTS

- - - - - - - - - - - -

Distressed leather boots have been having a major moment for years, but the style, made popular and done best by Frye, actually originated in 1863. The irreverent boots were worn by Civil War soldiers, and even Gold Rushers. They didn't become fashionable until almost a hundred years later—in the '60s, when women put the ultrafeminine heels away for a bit, aiming for a cooler, tough-girl look that's stuck around for years.

Ten Sneaky Tricks for
Nabbing Deals on Black Friday

1 **Make sure you're getting the lowest price.** If you see an ad for an in-store-only super-deal door-buster you want, search price comparison engines like PriceGrabber to make sure that the alleged deal is, in fact, the lowest available price.

2 **Shop from the bottom up.** When shopping on-line, hit View All and then shop from the bottom up of the sale page. Everyone else will be shopping top down so things sell out more quickly at the top of the page.

3 **Make a list** of who you need to buy gifts for on an organizing site like RememberTheMilk.com and check off when you score something for each one. This will help you focus, which is necessary when speed is of the essence.

4 **Use a fast browser.** We find Google Chrome to be the fastest at loading the page.

5 **Use an autofill tool** for your credit card and ship-ping address. You can set up tools like RoboForm to remember your passwords to your favorite sites and also fill in shipping addresses to various places.

6 Watch out for shipping charges. Sometimes the deal loses its allure if the shipping charges are as much as the product, so make sure you know how much it's going to be before you complete the check-out. You can save on shipping charges by using an unlimited free shipping service like ShopRunner.com, where you pay a flat fee for unlimited free two-day shipping on over a million products.

7 Make sure the items are in stock or guaranteed for holiday delivery; if not, you might be hand-ing out IOUs on December 25. We've had this happen personally, where a week after we made the purchase we were sent an email saying it was out of stock. We had to scramble for an alternative gift.

8 Know the return policy—some of the sale items may be final sale.

9 Get free shipping. Go to FreeShipping.org for a list of retailers offering free shipping. Keep in mind that some stores offer online purchase with in-store pickup. Search their policies or call customer service to find out.

10 Grab a promotional code. To find promotional codes, go to RetailMeNot.com or google the name of the shopping site with the words *coupon code* or *promotion code*.

HOW TO ORGANIZE YOUR CLOSET: FALL

The leaves are changing—everything is about warmth and hunkering down for a completely new season. While it happens slowly, pretty soon you'll be cranking the heat on in your home. No need to hibernate just yet, though: The weather is still fine—in fact, it's the most fun time of the year for fashion, because accessories really rule. Whereas summer dressing is all about making the most out of as little clothing as possible, we're giving you permission to pile on the layers without regret. First, keep your jackets around—if you've got a leather jacket, blazer or trench coat hidden away, it's time to pull it out again. Bring your closed-toe shoes—pumps, boots, booties, rain boots and flats—back into the fold if they still pass muster (look at the checklist on page 10 if you're unsure). Those cardigans, light sweaters and cozy knits will need to be put into service now, too, so hide your swimsuits and cover-ups for now (until you take a midwinter vacation, at least) and make room. If your layering pieces are still in great shape, like those tanks and tees you have, by all means, make a place for them, too—they'll be working hard this season. Jeans are the unofficial uniform for fall weekends, so find a pair that you love (see page 156) and buy them in a few different washes to keep it interesting. Keep those flirty, flowy dresses, and stock your underwear drawer with socks and new tights that aren't stretched out. Take a look at your leather handbags—if they're in good shape, make room for them, too.

MAKING THE CASE FOR . . .
the Tweed Jacket

We love a combination of irreverent and ladylike, so may we suggest adding a tweed jacket that's a little bit distressed, à la a messy, more complicated Coco Chanel? Wear it with jeans, black pants, pretty much everything. You'll be surprised how much you wear it. Try it with these three combinations.

EASY AS
1, 2, 3

1. Chain-strap handbag + button-down shirt + flats
2. Skinny jeans + tank top + driving moccasins
3. Leather skirt + printed top + booties

HOW TO TRANSITION YOUR SUMMER CLOTHES INTO FALL

The air is getting crisper, but that doesn't mean you have to put away your summer dresses. Here are our four creative ways to refashion your summer clothes with your fall additions so you can maximize what you've already got in your closet.

THE MAXI-DRESS

You wore your floor-length silk floral maxi to BBQs and beach parties during the summer. You don't have to say goodbye to it for fall.

FALL-IFY IT: Throw a chunky cardigan over it, add a belt and some booties, or go for a trench paired with thigh-high boots for nighttime.

THE LIGHTWEIGHT SWEATER

You threw it on while dining alfresco—now you can incorporate it into your fall wardrobe, too.

FALL-IFY IT: A thin, oversized sweater can look incredibly sexy when paired with a maxi-skirt, a mini-skirt or fall's best new jeans. Add a long pendant for more drama.

THE COLORFUL PENCIL SKIRT

You wore it to work with sandals all summer long—it brightened up all your drab neutrals.

FALL-IFY IT: Throw on a leather jacket and a pair of peep-toe booties for a pulled-together, edgy look.

WHITE JACKET

You bought it after Memorial Day to wear for all those summer meetings and cool spring nights. Well, guess what? You can wear it after Labor Day, too.

FALL-IFY IT: Pair it with your black cigarette pants and a pair of flats for casual Friday, layered over a black tank top and some colorful enamel bangles.

a Summer Scarf through Fall

We love the beginning of autumn, when it's too cool to sweat and too warm to wear a jacket. That's why keeping the scarf you've been wearing on chillier summer nights is always a good idea. You don't really want to break out a sweater just yet.

Start with a lighter-colored cotton scarf in plaid—appropriate for fall yet not too wintery. We like updating the scarf from summer to autumn with booties and slim dark denim, and then adding a white henley. (A couple of the shirt's top buttons can be unfastened, so the scarf can sit both on and inside the henley.) Add a long-strap shoulder bag in a warm fall color, a metallic leather wrap bracelet, and you're good to go.

FASHIONMATH:
Is a Proenza Schouler Satchel Worth the High Cost?

We're in love with the Proenza Schouler PS1 satchel (retail: $1,995). The rich, soft leather bag is not only gorgeous, but convertible: With a cross-body strap and handle, it's like two handbags in one.

Since the hefty price tag is comparable to a down payment on a compact car, perhaps a little fashion math will help justify it:

$$\{ \text{\$1,995 divided by 365 days of envy} = \text{\$5.47/wear} \}$$

If you carried this bag every day for the next year, it amounts to about $6 a day—less than a blended Starbucks drink and a scone, but still more than a regular coffee. If you have expensive taste, you know that a great bag actually lasts for years—so the per diem is even less than $6. We're known as fashion enablers among our friends, so we may not be a voice of reason here, but we say it's a sound investment.

HOW TO FIND JEANS THAT FIT

Hate hearing the waiflike dressing-room attendant yell, "Do you need a bigger size?!" We hear you. There's more to finding a great pair of jeans than trying on a thousand pairs in the dressing room. Jump-start your search by narrowing down your options. Because, honestly, who has the time to troll the racks, wait for a dressing room, struggle to maneuver all those pairs of pants on and off, and then spend even more precious minutes in line for the register? Take the guesswork out of the whole task by figuring out what works for you beforehand.

THE WAIST: A medium to high waist helps flatten your tummy, limit the peeking thong and reduce the muffin top. And a high waist, contrary to popular belief, can be very flattering for lengthening legs, creating a curvier derriere and slimming the thighs.

THE SHAPE: Slim fits are best left for the skinny-legged gals of the world. Those with fuller thighs will appreciate the balancing act of wide-legged jeans, boot-cut styles and slim flares.

THE FABRIC: Large hips, butts and thighs benefit from Lycra, which reduces a gaping waist. In fact, for most girls, even a little bit of forgiveness can make all the difference between a pair of jeans you hide in the back of your closet and the ones that hug just perfectly. As for details (like extra pockets), if you're thinner, the more, the better. If you want to camouflage a few pounds, fewer details mean more slimming action.

THE COLOR: The darker the wash, the slimmer your legs will look. Likewise, a solid, all-over wash will do more to lengthen than sand washing. On the contrary, if you are thin and want to add curves, you could look for jeans that are lighter around the thighs and rear.

THE LENGTH: Grab a tape measure and check your inseam while wearing the shoes with which you plan to wear the jeans. This gives you insight into the proper jean length you need to wear them perfectly. And for taller girls, seek out jeans with about a thirty-six-inch inseam.

HOW TO WEAR . . .
Spots—Everything from Leopard to Crocodile

Leopard print, when done right, can be extremely chic, à la Ann-Margret and Sophia Loren. Don't be afraid to take a walk on the wild side. Here's how to pull off the animal print look so no one mistakes you for Snooki.

1 Scale animal prints to your size. Tighter prints, like cheetah and leopard, look great on most people. Larger-scale prints, like cow or giraffe, have lots of white space in them and are more difficult to pull off, so best to try them in smaller accessories, like belts, shoes or smaller handbags.

2 Pair animal prints with neutrals (black, khaki, camel, cream, white) and they'll always be in style.

3 If you want to try leopard in a big, statement-making way, we love a leopard look in fall. The rest of your ensemble should be understated, though.

4 Remember that you'll be calling attention to wherever you put the animal prints, so make sure you're putting it on your best feature (no printed pants on big bottoms or tight-print tops on large busts).

5 If you want to ease into leopard, try a lining inside a coat or bag or choose a great pair of shoes with just a touch of leopard as an accent so it's not overpowering.

TECH EFFECT:
THE BEST SITES TO BUY JEANS
(ONE MORE PAIR WON'T HURT)

Denim shopping is intimidating enough in a dressing room (that light, ugh!), so making the switch to a virtual store can be positively scary. Don't worry—we're here to help. We've browsed and tested thousands of denim sites to bring you the best of the best when it comes to helping you score that perfect pair of jeans.

Shopbop: The most extensive collection.
Buyers scour known and little-known brands to bring the best selection available to their customers. From Rag and Bone to Levi's to Current/Elliott, Shopbop has an enviable list of drool-worthy brands. They also offer video fit guides for all the brands they carry, so you can see how they move.

Piperlime: Free shipping, free returns, one-year return policy.
Piperlime (a Gap spinoff brand) seems to understand jeans are a tough sell online since sizes run differently in each brand—and sometimes you really just have to try them on to see if they work for your body. Free shipping, free returns and a one-year return policy make it easier to find the right fit at this site.

Revolve Clothing: Find the next big denim designer.

Revolve Clothing is like your cool girlfriend who always looks effortlessly chic. With a keen eye for indie brands like Black Orchid, Bleulab (they're reversible!) and Mother, Revolve finds jeans that everyone is going to want. Each pair comes with its own fit guide tab, plus the site has free ground shipping and free returns.

Wash Away: Your Guide to Denim Washes, Once and for All

Light washes: Best for casual daytime weekends, when you're running errands or hanging around the house. We prefer a boyfriend style with some distressing for a casual look that makes you look tiny. Wear with a white button-down shirt or a fitted tee.

Medium washes: Still a little bit on the casual side, these can be paired with flats to go for lunch, or on errands, like shopping, or playdates with your kids or to the farmers' market.

Dark washes: Perfect for casual Friday in the office, dark washes are the dressiest wash. These are at their best at night when paired with your sexiest heels and a black top. Plus, they're super-slimming on everyone. Who can't get behind that?

SEASONAL SOS

SOLUTIONS FOR FALL
FASHION EMERGENCIES

It's Indian summer in the daytime, but winds blow through after the sun sets.

SOLUTION: Keep two things in your bag always—a camel cashmere or cashmerelike shawl that can double as a scarf and a thin cashmerelike or merino wool black cardigan. This way you can wear short sleeves to the office when it's warm and then layer on the sweater and shawl as the temps drop.

You're in the mood to wear your new fall clothes, but it's still over seventy-five degrees out.

SOLUTION: Wear lightweight layers in a deep color palette. Get some tees in dark brown, heather gray and deep red. You can pair them with a tropical-weight wool skirt or pants and keep cool.

You love the look of a crisp button-down shirt for work, but you end up busting out of it.

SOLUTIONS: Fashion tape. These strips stay stuck all day, and when you take off your shirt for washing, just remove the strip and throw it away. Get a pack of ten for under $5, or order five packs and get free shipping. We found them at PrivacyStrips.com. Simply apply the strip to the inside of your button-down blouse and you'll never have to fear that onlookers might be getting a glance you'd rather not have them see. Another option that we suggest for women who constantly wear button-down shirts, and who can't ever seem to find one that fits correctly, is to buy your shirts a size bigger. Make sure that when you purchase them there's no gaping at the bust whatsoever. Then take your shirts to a professional tailor who can bring in the waist to fit your body. It may cost more initially, but you'll have a perfect fit every time.

Yes, They *Do* Exist . . .

We both love the classic look of a white button down, which is perpetually on every "must have" list, but it's been impossible to find one to fit our chests without looking sloppy. Until now. There are two companies that specifically make shirts for women who need more room in the bosom area, finally! "The Shirt" by Rochelle Behrens, created especially for girls who have a common problem—they can't wear a button-down shirt without busting out of it; and Rebecca & Drew, a company that smartly makes shirts according to height, cup size and chest circumference.

Booties, without Looking Stout

Booties, unlike their knee-high cousins, can shorten the leg. If you're svelte, no worries, but if your legs aren't your best attribute, make sure to buy ankle boots that hit just above the ankle or shoe boots that hit right below the ankle. Styles that stop right at the ankle bone will interfere with the line of the leg. Also, avoid long skirts or short, fitted ones that can make your legs look out of proportion. Midthigh to knee-length A-line styles, which leave room to breathe, are great, as well as sweater dresses and A-line dresses.

Stay warm: Tights are a must. If you really fear your shape, wear leggings. Black makes everything look slimmer and will hide all imperfections. It's the one advantage of cold weather!

Forget pants: Unless they are slim-fit, can be rolled up or tucked into the tops of the booties, opt for skirts or dresses, rather than pants.

Comfort first: No matter how hot your boots are, it's important that they're comfortable on your feet. So steer clear of six-inch heels unless you're a pro.

FASHION STORMS: STAY STYLISH NO MATTER HOW FICKLE THE WEATHER

Seasonal transitions can send your closet into a tizzy. In September you haven't rotated in the serious sweaters because it's still balmy during the day, but then when the sun goes down the temperature plummets. The key to this time of year is layers. One of the most chic looks is the little jacket with a big, bright cashmere scarf looped around your neck. Take a T-shirt, add a thin sweater, pile on a wool blazer or leather jacket and you'll be set no matter what the temperature. During this season we also keep an emergency pair of tights stashed in our office drawer should we be caught bare-legged for a sudden change in the forecast.

FALL STYLE CONUNDRUMS: WHAT TO WEAR . . .

TO THE REUNION

Who were you in high school? The popular cheerleader, the jock, the drama geek or the loner who ate lunch crouched in a bathroom stall? Wait until your classmates see you now. Whether you have something to prove or just can't wait to reunite with your childhood pals, you've got to look good. Don't be the one everyone walks away gossiping about. Time to dress to impress! While you

EASY AS
1, 2, 3

1. Bold bright sleeve-
   less sheath +
   patent-leather belt
   + envelope clutch

2. Black sequin tank
   dress + black
   satin vest + chain-
   strap bag

3. Metallic dress in
   subdued silver,
   pewter and bronze
   + nude shoes +
   cross-body bag

don't have to arrive in a helicopter à la *Romy and Michelle's High School Reunion*, we *do* recommend pulling out all the stops for your reunion. Keep the venue in mind, though: You don't want to show up in a ball gown at a dive bar, obviously.

Here's where we recommend using Rent the Runway, our favorite site for renting a runway dress for much less (see page 197 for more information). We'd go for something drapey (no need to diet for months) and colorful—even if you were a wallflower in high school, now's the time to stand out and strut your stuff.

APPLE PICKING

It's such a quintessentially fall activity to spend the day surrounded by apple trees and farm-grown treats like apple cider and homemade pies. Head out to the orchards in something comfortable—high-maintenance chicks need not apply here—you're actually going to be working to some extent, but you'll get something out of it! Try skinny cargo pants (the more pockets to fill with your goods!) or comfortable skinny jeans with sneakers by Tretorn, Bensimon or Superga and a pair of sunglasses. We prefer

EASY AS
1, 2, 3

1. V-neck tee **+** skinny cargo pants **+** denim jacket

2. Long-sleeved henley **+** skinny jeans **+** puffy vest

3. Lightweight dress **+** tights **+** belted wool oversized cardigan

aviators, because they work with every face shape and are timeless (see page 114 for more). This is a great opportunity to pull out that down vest you've been hiding in your closet—you'll need your arms free for all of that inevitable reaching. Layer it over a knit sweater or a long-sleeved top and stuff a hat in your pocket for later. You'll need the coverage once the sun starts to set.

TO THE FOOTBALL GAME

It's a quintessentially American pastime, so it's best to go classic here. Our biggest pet peeve at a sporting event is when spectators dress like they should be *in* the game. Please, don't make this mistake. Sweatpants and track pants are out. Don't dress like a cheerleader. (Trust us, we've seen it: It's never as cute as you think it is.) If you'd be embarrassed to walk into a restaurant in your getup, you probably should think twice about wearing it to the game.

Throw on a pair of your most flattering jeans, because it doesn't get more American than a great-fitting, butt-hugging pair of blues. If you have a team T-shirt and want to show some pride, layer it underneath a cozy pullover sweater—the more distressed the team shirt, the cooler it'll look. And if the sun comes out, you can wear it alone. We think this way is cooler than layering under your team tee, as in a turtleneck or collared shirt, which tends to make most people look like they're on a school field trip.

Remember, you'll be sitting in one place for most of the game, so you might want to layer with a button-down shirt in a cozy flannel or chambray. Bring along a small bag like a cross-body bag that doesn't require a lot of looking after—you can just sling it across your arms. We'd wear either flat boots or moccasins or sneakers to make the climb through the bleachers up to the nosebleed seats easier. And don't forget the sunscreen—or the sunglasses!

TO FASHION WEEK

Despite its name, Fashion Week actually goes on for *several* weeks, and the biggest, most hyped blocks of shows happen in New York City, Milan and Paris, the fashion capitals of the world. If you score an invitation, you'll find yourself in the same room as the most renowned designers, models and editors from around the world.

There's no need to buy a designer item to wear to Fashion Week just because you landed an invitation. It's all about the way you put your clothes together, and the more confident you appear during the shows and at the parties that surround them, the better.

If you're going to attend shows at Fashion Week, be aware that you will be judged, so make sure to edit your wardrobe accordingly. Pay close attention to fabrics, first of all. Go for gorgeous fabrics, and a mix of textures and finishes (satin, patent leather, metallic, etc.).

Most importantly, interpret the trends for your body, not just because they're "in" right now. It's always better to dress for your body than to follow the latest fad any day. Throw on a leather jacket over a dress in a luxe fabric, whether it's silk, chiffon or brocade, push up the sleeves, add a belt that pops, a pair of sky-high pumps and a fistful of bangles and you'll fit right in. As a general rule, wear your most spectacular accessories: camel coat, brightly colored leather handbag and chicest heels, and one impressive jewelry piece—extra points if it's vintage. If you're sitting in the front row and you own something the designer has created, by all means, wear it, and garner some fashion brownie points. You never know where it could get you.

EASY AS

1, 2, 3

1. Leather jacket + silk printed dress + booties

2. Vintage statement necklace + bold colorful dress + strappy stilettos

3. Brocade skirt + silk top + over-the-knee leather boots

PART III

YOUR FASHION CALENDER

WHAT TO WEAR FOR ANY—AND EVERY— OCCASION

CHAPTER 7

Holidays & Observances
WHAT TO WEAR WHEN

With all the craziness surrounding the holidays—what with the presents and guest lists and errands to run—it's often too late before you realize you actually need to figure out your outfit for the day. We're here to help. Anytime you're at a loss, come back to this chapter again for ideas on what to wear for your holiday parties.

NEW YEAR'S EVE

Ringing in the New Year—the parties, the bubbly, the sparkle! After this night, the holidays are over—you'll likely spend the next day nursing your hangover, so we recommend going out with a bang, and that means sky-high heels, your most fabulous dress and a positive attitude. No matter what happens, even if the party you're attending doesn't live up the hype that surrounds it, you'll look amazing, and isn't that the most important part?

This is absolutely not the time to wear your trusty little black dress. Be a little more daring, for goodness sake—everyone in the world is celebrating tonight, so join the party with a dramatic ensemble. Tonight is your excuse to dress like an A-list movie star, even if you're more of a couch potato most of the year.

IF YOU'RE MORE OF A JEANS-AND-T-SHIRT KIND OF GIRL

If pants are more your thing, don't shove yourself into a cocktail dress—you won't have fun because you won't feel like yourself, so be true to your style, just punch it up a little. Throw on some black satin pants, or layer tights with evening shorts (whether they're shimmery, sequin or brocade, make sure they stand out) and pile on a gorgeous evening jacket, some long necklaces and high heels. If you truly do not want to part with your jeans, make them work with your look—go for dark or black denim, a pair of stilettos, and something a little excessive up top, like a fur coat.

IF YOU'VE GOT SOME LEGS TO SHOW OFF

Remember, dressing is all about balance (see page 23 for more on this), so if you're going to show off your incredible legs, go for a micro-mini in a fun print. If you must wear black, make sure the cocktail dress is textured, whether that means a feather skirt or beaded straps—this is not the time to be a wallflower! Go for high heels, and if you live in a cold-weather locale, make sure the tights are new—the better to start a new year—and maybe even fleece lined, if it's super-cold. Consider a fur (faux or otherwise) jacket and don't forget the jewelry—whether that means lots of sparkly bangles or one killer pair of earrings.

PLAY IT FAST AND LOOSE

- - - - - - - - - - -

Don't go too stodgy on the hair if your attire is formal—if you're going to rock the night away, might as well wear it long and loose and keep the makeup sultry.

IF YOU'RE THE BELLE OF THE BALL

Say it's your party or, maybe this year, you're invited to a black-tie event in an out-of-this world locale—you've gotta go full-on ball gown. Just make sure to keep it fresh. If your gown is long and black, go for a plunging neckline or a strapless number. Show those shoulders off, and wear some super-sparkly chandelier earrings. If it's super-formal, you might even consider some long gloves to complement your dress. When else do you have an excuse to wear them?

EASY AS

1, 2, 3

1. Sequin top +
   black satin pants
   + evening jacket
2. Chiffon cocktail
   dress + fur vest +
   contrasting shoes
3. Ball gown + gloves
   + sparkly jewelry

NEW YEAR'S DAY: THE BRUNCH

New Year's Day brunch is one of those rituals that practically everyone in the world can revel in. As the last day of vacation, it is truly a day of rest and relaxation. It should be renamed National Hangover Day, considering the exorbitant amount of eggs Benedict consumed worldwide. After a night of partying hard, you deserve to take some time to restore your energies. Here's what you need to put together a great New Year's Day brunch outfit without straining that champagne-induced hangover. We lay ours out the night before so we don't even have to think.

Choose a sweater that's warm and cuddly, whether it's a cashmere blend or wool with toggles. Fair Isle sweaters can look especially chic

EASY AS
1, 2, 3

1. Oversized cashmere sweater **+** black skinny jeans **+** flat boots
2. Embellished tunic **+** ponté pants **+** flats
3. Fair Isle sweater **+** distressed boyfriend jeans **+** moccasins

when paired with distressed jeans, a brown leather belt and riding boots or flats. Today is all about comfort, but if you even try to wear sweatpants to a restaurant, we'll come and find you. (Sometimes we wish the fashion police actually existed!) You've got to start the new year in style, so throw on your most comfortable skinny pants—ponté pants (see "Get a Leg Up," below) offer room and are often stretchy enough without looking like workout pants (even though they feel like them!). After a night of dancing in stilettos, you deserve to give your feet a break. Throw on a pair of flat shoes with support, like a pair of suede moccasins or flat boots.

Get a Leg Up

If you desperately want to wear leggings, but don't feel comfortable wearing them in public, Paige Denim makes amazing jeanlike ponté pants called Verduro jeggings that have actual pockets and a button closure, but they feel just like jersey leggings. Pull on some flat leather boots. You've got the best of both worlds . . . no worrying about popping a button.

VALENTINE'S DAY

It may be a Hallmark holiday, but you've got to admit, it's a great excuse to dress up a little—whether you have a hot date or are headed out for a wild night with your single girlfriends, even if it's just to the movie theater to watch the latest cheesefest chick flick or art house drama. This is a great chance to play up your best assets and look sexy. Instead of red, which every other woman is going to be wearing tonight, try a monochromatic look of soft pastels by mixing creamy lace, airy florals and nude shoes. If it's cold in your city, pair these with black tights—it's a gorgeous combination we don't see enough of!

EASY AS
1, 2, 3

1. Jeans **+** silk top **+** over-the-knee boots

2. Cutout dress **+** hoop earrings **+** heels

3. Sequin or fringe dress **+** leather gloves **+** studded belt

IF YOU'RE HANGING WITH YOUR FRIENDS . . .

Wear what makes you feel good about yourself. As you know, girls really just dress for each other anyway, so wear your best-fitting jeans, a silk or dolman-sleeve top, and your most fun jewelry, whether it's your biggest hoops, or chunkiest bangles. Over-the-knee leather boots are always sexy, so throw them on and you'll forget all about not having a date.

IF YOU'RE GOING TO A PARTY . . .

Play up your assets in a short dress with a flattering line for your body (see page 23) or embellishment, like a black sequin dress with fringe. Sexy heels are a must, and might we suggest you spice things up even more with a cool belt? (See page 30 for some ideas.) It's all about keeping things interesting. Want to stand out from the pack? Then absolutely do not wear red, but red, pink or coral lipstick can be extremely chic if you're in the mood for it.

IF YOU HAVE A DATE . . .

Don't buy into the hype: Just go out and have a fun night with your guy. The key is to look sexy without going overboard, so play up your best assets in a body-conscious dress, whether that means a cutout dress (see page 271 on bachelorette parties for more on these), an Herve Leger bandage dress or a Diane von Furstenberg wrap dress. Find what works for your body. Wear a sentimental piece of jewelry, preferably one he gave you, not something from an ex-boyfriend, and a hot pair of your strappiest, sexiest heels—your guy will check you out all night long.

EASTER/PASSOVER

This is a great time to break out a spring sundress in a pastel or floral print. You don't have to look like an Easter egg, but everything is more fun when you get in the spirit. Pastels and khakis can be very flattering on nearly all women— just brush on some bronzer and slick on some pink gloss so you don't look washed out. If you're going to church or temple, make sure you've got a cardigan sweater or a khaki trench coat (see page 90 for our favorites) to go along with it. If it's chilly, as it often is, choose a pair of wide-leg khakis with a silk floral top tucked in and a cropped jacket or sweater to complete the look. Wear a pair of flats or wedges to stay comfortable on your feet during all the activities that follow—prayer, family dinner, seder, Easter egg hunts in the grass, and awkward conversations with your grandmother about why you don't have a boyfriend/when you're having a baby/why you don't visit her often enough.

Outfit in a Pinch

You got invited to celebrate Easter or Passover with your new boyfriend and you have nothing to wear? Tuck a white cotton or lace blouse or a white button-down shirt into a bright A-line skirt, add a pair of wedges or even embellished flats, plus a classic khaki trench. Extra credit if you add a belt. Whether it's glittery, metallic or contrasting, it can make the outfit look fresh and vibrant, not thrown together. Phew!

MEMORIAL DAY

We always try to get away this weekend, even if we can only swing it for a day or two. It's the unofficial commencement of summer—and aren't you excited to start dressing like it? First of all, invest in a giant tote to carry with you everywhere—try sunny colors mixed with neutrals (like yellow and khaki or coral and gray) and carry everything you'll need for events on a moment's notice. Stash extra sunblock, bottled water, a bikini and your beach read. Banish

your slimming blacks, and go for the more nautical (but still ultraslimming) navy and purples. Get a bright pedicure, grab your sunglasses, a pair of sandals and espadrilles, a few tanks and cardigans, a pair of tailored navy trousers for cool nights, and a sundress or two if your legs are ready to bare. Now get thyself to a barbecue with a swipe of bronzer and have a burger along with a few celebratory drinks. Cheers.

EASY AS
1, 2, 3

1. Slim navy pants + striped tank + straw hat

2. Bikini + printed cover-up + flat sandals

3. Bright summer dress + lightweight cardigan + pendant necklace

INDEPENDENCE DAY

America's birthday is one of our favorite holidays. Summer is in full swing, which means the possibilities for relaxing and sun-soaked fun are endless. Pool parties, fireworks, flags and fireflies—it's all about partying all day with friends and truly celebrating the season. The key is to dress with versatility, which means lightweight cotton or linen pants or a pair of madras with a clean and crisp button-down shirt or a brightly colored shift dress, a cute pair of espadrilles and, if there's a pool or beach, bring a swimsuit, a towel and a change of underwear. If you're at the beach, consider bringing along a white denim jacket or linen pullover—it could get chilly.

EASYAS
1, 2, 3

1. Madras print skirt **+** sleeveless button-down top **+** chunky chain-link necklace

2. Linen sleeveless dress **+** lightweight scarf **+** straw hat

3. Shirt dress **+** belt **+** espadrilles

LABOR DAY

How did it go by so fast? Summer's last hurrah is here—plan a getaway, or at least a get-together with your friends, and really enjoy the last few hours of summer today. The leaves are starting to turn and your thoughts have started to turn to going back to work or school. On the upside, you can start thinking about fall wardrobes, too. But before you trade in your sandals for booties, show off that glowing tan you've worked on all season in a gorgeous white sheath dress or white wide-leg sailor pants with a chic sweater tank and flat sandals. Tie on a bright scarf as a headband or around your neck, pack your sunglasses and bring along a beach tote for all the day's essentials. Whether you're on your way to a pool party or a picnic, be sure to take a moment to enjoy it.

EASY AS
1, 2, 3

1. White shirt dress
+ gauzy cardigan
+ distressed
leather belt

2. White linen
pants + striped
or embellished
tank + wedges

3. Scarf + printed
sleeveless dress +
flat sandals

HALLOWEEN

This is one of our favorite holidays—it's the one day of the year where you can dress as whomever (or whatever) you want. But choose wisely! Depending on what you have planned, your costume can either be a hit or a really big miss. And, as we've cautioned before, with Facebook being so prevalent, a photo of you in your costume is bound to turn up eventually, so don't dress in anything you'd be embarrassed about (i.e., anything too slutty or scandalous), especially if your boss or parents have access to your page. While you could always put your own spin on some of the more conventional costumes, like witches, policewomen, nurses, black cats or pirates, you could also push the envelope. A great rule of thumb is to pay attention to pop-culture icons all year round. If you see a popular movie and love the style of one of the characters, consider creating a costume around it. Make sure you're comfortable before leaving the house. If you feel your dress is too revealing or you think, even for one second, that you might be embarrassed, consider tweaking your costume a bit. We promise, you'll never regret that your costume wasn't slutty enough.

Some of the most clever costumes we've ever seen are:

+ Gold diggers
+ Pop stars
+ Cartoon couples
+ Reality stars
+ Celebrity couples
+ Cult-following TV drama costumes

The worst costumes we've ever seen include:

+ Bloody tampons
+ Hot tranny messes
+ Train wrecks
+ Britney Spears in her head-shaving phase
+ Zombie brides

The common theme here is that all these costumes are gross, and require you to look like a hot mess. Halloween comes once a year—wouldn't you rather dress up?

THANKSGIVING

It's the beginning of what will soon feel like an endless onslaught of holiday get-togethers. In some ways it feels completely novel: The leaves have just started to turn that golden shade, the weather is getting a little bit crisp and, hey, you get the day off to spend stuffing your face with turkey. The stress about holiday gifts has yet to kick in. Save that until tomorrow, on Black Friday, and see our tips on page 148 for getting through it unscathed. For now, consider your location. Are you going to your parents' house to dine with your siblings, aunts, uncles and cousins? Dress according to your companions. If your family is casual, consider wearing a smart pair of slacks, and a silk tie top with flats. Or maybe your dining companions are a little more festive: Throw on your little black (navy, brown or camel-colored) dress, a pair of tights to stave off the chill and a pair of boots. Today is all about being thankful, so don't stress too much about it. If you're meeting your boyfriend's parents for the first time on Thanksgiving, skip to page 219 for our advice on what to wear. It's a toughie, we know!

EASY AS
1, 2, 3

1. Trousers **+** silk tie top **+** flats
2. Little black dress **+** tights **+** flat boots
3. Lace dress **+** sparkly earrings **+** booties

FASHIONMATH:
Is It Worth Investing in Pearls?

A pearl necklace will always be classic, thanks to fashion mavens like Jackie O, Coco Chanel and Michelle Obama. Time and time again, we see pearl necklaces adorn the necks of elegant women, but can never tell the difference between the faux and the real deal. Once we started actually looking into buying pearl necklaces for ourselves, though, we understood. There's a huge difference between faux and real pearls when you try them on: The weight of them, even the sheen, is different. But we found a four-strand pearl necklace we had to invest in, and it cost $325. So what did we do? The fashion math, of course.

> **$325 divided by 90 ladylike days and nights = $3.61/wear**

One wear of this necklace is the same price as your daily coffee. Three months out of the year you are bound to grab this staple—made with freshwater pearls and hand-knotted on silk thread. The strands' varying lengths and sizes make a modern statement, and you can wear this necklace for formal *and* casual events. Do you want to be known as the grandmother who passed along the cheap pearls? Didn't think so.

CHRISTMAS/
HANUKKAH/KWANZAA

Now is the time to kick your wardrobe up a notch, not play it safe. As the holiday party invites flow in, invest in a few accessories to carry even the most limited wardrobe from cocktails to a night at the opera. Leave the red and white to Santa, and avoid looking like an elf in head-to-toe red and green. The last thing you need is for everyone to be sneering the next day about your misguided "festive attire."

All the upcoming holiday soirees (with photos posted afterwards, of course) warrant one stand-alone sparkly and festive accessory to go along with your perfect party dress. See below for a few of our favorite holiday accessories—the more sparkly and bright, the better, we say.

A statement necklace, meaning something that people will notice. If you're conservative, go the safe route with pearls, but make them big pearls. We recommend the more daring rhinestones or chunky gold or silver chains. A stunning pendant is also an option. You don't have to spend a mint. Etsy.com is an amazing site for one-of-a-kind handmade or vintage baubles that will give your little black dress some zing. Insider tip: We love BaubleBar.com, a site that sells cool jewelry (without disclosing the brand names) for way less. Genius, right?

A pair of party heels that make you want to dance (i.e., embellished with satin, bows or rhinestones).

A cool evening clutch. Look for exotics, metallics and luxe fabrics like silk in bright colors. A pop of an unexpected color is the perfect antidote to an all-gray or black outfit, but can just as easily make navy blue, emerald green or winter white look a little more fashion-forward.

A Note on Fur

While real fur was considered extremely chic and luxurious until the late 1970s, it's not necessary to wear the real thing in order to make a big impression. Faux fur has become acceptable, even preferred, in many fashion circles, and you can find it everywhere from QVC to Chanel. Wear a faux fur vest with your cocktail dress, or throw a faux mink stole over your look, fastened with a vintage brooch. PETA will thank you.

HOW TO CHOOSE YOUR
PERFECT HOLIDAY PARTY DRESS

Kick up your normal routine with a little bit of glamour. For holiday party dresses, get the best mileage out of neutrals like black, gray and bronzes with precious details—and watch the compliments fly.

If You're a Stick-to-Neutrals Girl . . .

Change things up with the shape of your dress—like a strapless version with blocks of color, or a longsleeved body-con number.

If You Like Drama . . .

Go for a flowy A-line dress with a retro nod, like a full skirt in a royal blue, yellow or gold brocade that will add some fun to your look.

If You Like Sparkles . . .

Try a matte sequin in a gunmetal shade, or a little black dress with some embellishment, like a built-in beaded collar or a sequin trim.

You can't go wrong with something fun and a little bit sparkly—so use this as your excuse to take that embellished dress, the crocodile clutch or the ginormous cocktail ring out of the closet for a spin. It's a party—really, anything goes. If all else fails, just remember: Eggnog has a funny way of making people forget.

EASY AS
1, 2, 3

1. Satin A-line dress + fur shrug + chandelier earrings
2. Matte sequin dress + clutch + cocktail ring
3. Silk shell + satin voluminous skirt + belt

CHAPTER 8

Survival Year-Round
SIMPLE WARDROBE SOLUTIONS
FOR FASHION STORMS

The weather may be unpredictable, but your fashion life doesn't have to be. We've anticipated any—and every—possible miscellaneous fashion storm, so whatever the situation, we've got you covered, in style (but that was a given).

A BLACK-TIE AFFAIR

We get more questions about black-tie affairs than almost anything else (except how to find the best bra, which we tackle on page 27). The two words *black tie*, most commonly embossed on hard stock paper in curly script, seem to send even the most fashionably assured women into a panic. It doesn't have to be that way! Think of it like this: Black tie is a way to let you wear your fanciest coat, gloves, necklace . . . all the stuff that takes a back seat to your everyday wardrobe—anything you would "save for a special occasion." Just do it tastefully. Black-tie affairs are elegant soirees, so you don't want to wear anything too outlandish. If your job or your social life requires you to attend one or two black-tie affairs a year, then invest in a long, black strapless, one-shoulder or V-neck gown, and add your most fabulous shoes and your own jewelry to it. And if you don't have any rich relatives, who left you heirlooms in their wills, let vintage pieces you pick up on Etsy, eBay or Portero add a little more zing to your look. No one will balk at a big honking diamond necklace or a cocktail ring—that's what black tie is, by definition—just keep it elegant and don't go too crazy with the color. If you're bored with black, try jewel tones—emerald, sapphire or opal—they're timeless and always look luxe enough for a black-tie night out on the town. If it's cold, bring along a fur shrug, or a coat you wouldn't wear every day. If it's a more fashion-forward crowd, don't be afraid of bright colors, like cobalt blue or coral, as long as they've got some sort of luxe detailing, like draping, or your gown is a cool backless number. It's all about bringing out your best stuff tonight. Just don't forget to remove those elbow-length gloves while they're passing around the hors d'oeuvres.

EASY AS
1, 2, 3

1. Jewel-toned gown + layered jewel necklace + elbow-length gloves

2. One-shoulder ruffle gown + long earrings + satin clutch

3. Floor-length gown in a light fabric with a print + hoop earrings + stilettos

Why Buy a Bunch of Dresses You'll Wear Only Once, When You Can Rent Them?

Whether you're a sorority girl going to mixers every weekend, your job requires you to attend a lot of cocktail parties or you have a ton of weddings to go to this year, make friends with our favorite rental site, Rent the Runway. Like Netflix for dresses, the site lets you borrow everything from super high-end gowns to clutches to jewelry for four to eight days. When the time's up, you won't turn into a pumpkin: Just put the goods in the prepaid package in the mail and you're done. They do the dry cleaning and you don't go broke— or worse, commit the cardinal sin of leaving the tags on a dress and then returning it. No worries about sizing: You can get two sizes sent to you just in case you're unsure about how a specific designer fits. If it doesn't fit, you can get a refund. If you want to rent some really stunning diamonds, Adorn.com lets you do it—with a similar business model as Rent the Runway, but for jewels. You'll feel like an A-lister in Adorn's sparkling pieces. No one has to know you didn't inherit them.

A JOB INTERVIEW AT A PLACE WITH A STRICT DRESS CODE

When in doubt, wear a suit. Yes, even if it's pouring rain or the muggiest of summer days. If you discover that you're wildly overdressed, you can always remove your jacket—as long as the top underneath isn't too revealing. Wearing a suit is particularly important if you have a young-looking face and prefer to appear experienced and reliable, not fresh out of college.

You can't go wrong with basic black. The fail-safe choice in any situation is a black suit. It's always appropriate and matches everything. Every professional woman should own at least one well-fitting black suit (pants or a just-below-the-knee skirt). If you're on an entry-level budget, the bonus is that less expensive fabrics look better in black than lighter colors.

Accessorize (cautiously). The place to show your personality is with accessories: a chunky necklace, a scarf-belt in a trendy fabric, a splurge-worthy tote, fabulous (closed-toe) shoes. But skip the jingly bracelets. They get in the way when you're making that super-important, first-impression handshake.

Overall, avoid having any element of your appearance make a bigger first impression than you do. It's hard enough to get a job and get ahead; never, ever lose an opportunity because of what you're wearing.

SHOES AND THE JOB INTERVIEW

When it comes to job interviews, first impressions are everything. In order to look pulled together and professional from head to toe, office-appropriate shoes are a must. Shoes should reflect you, but don't need to scream personal style à la Elle Woods's pink stilettos, nor should they be completely boring and basic. One rule that is not to be broken: Show no toes. Save your pedicure for after you've got the gig.

Professional Pumps

Pumps give you that extra boost (literally and figuratively) when you need all your confidence. They automatically dress up any otherwise simple outfit. That being said, subtlety is key: Simple feminine touches, inconspicuous studs or grommets, and simple buckles make the shoe eye-catching without being too splashy.

Flats with Flare

Job interviews are stressful enough: You don't want to add to your nerves by worrying about tipping over in heels. If you're not exactly runway-ready in stilettos, a clever flat is a good option. Choose flats in basic colors like black, brown or gray that have a little something extra. Bow detailing, a jeweled add-on or a textured fabric will make you a standout candidate.

These Boots Were Made for Interviewin'

Rules of thumb when wearing boots to meet a potential employer: No patent leather, nothing that goes over the knee, no bright colors, and don't add fishnets or crazy patterned tights. For knee-skimming boots, a pointy toe works well under dressy pants or with a knee-length pencil skirt. Stay away from cutouts or any kind of metallic booties. No need to go overboard with accents and detailing—remember that boots are enough of a statement on their own.

A JOB INTERVIEW
AT A CASUAL WORKPLACE

Even if you're going for a job at a notoriously casual workplace, where employees routinely wear sweatshirts and flip-flops to work, you should still dress up for the interview. In this case, it's okay if you're better-dressed than the person interviewing you. Just keep the look effortless: Don't wear a suit or it'll look like you won't fit in in their casual atmosphere. That said, a sheath and a fun (read: not pearl) necklace and a brightly colored pair of pumps work, or a printed skirt, cardigan and silk button-down are just as great. Leave the briefcase at home in favor of a large tote, big enough for your portfolio, in leather or an exotic skin, and you're on your way to scoring the gig. Work it, girl!

EASY AS
1, 2, 3

1. Printed skirt **+** silk button-down **+** leather portfolio

2. Colorful sheath **+** arty necklace **+** pumps

3. Layered bangles **+** ponté pants **+** blazer

EASY AS
1, 2, 3

1. Printed wrap dress + heels + statement necklace
2. Colorful or printed blouse + pencil skirt + blazer
3. Tie-front blouse + wide-leg trousers + loafer pumps

A BUSINESS LUNCH

The point of a business lunch is to build a more personal relationship with someone you want to do business with. Keep this in mind when you're getting dressed. Unless your industry mandates suits, you want to dress in something that shows a bit more personality. We like printed wrap dresses for these occasions. They're less stiff than a suit and the prints add a bit of fun to the atmosphere.

THE *BIG* WORK MEETING, OR WHEN PRESENTING AT A CONFERENCE

Your outfit to kill in the boardroom or on the dais needs to look sharp and sophisticated, but not take away from what you have to say. We believe in looking feminine while also taking your rightful seat at the big boys' table. We like a tailored red sheath dress with a blazer over it and classic jewelry like pearls, diamond studs or a delicate bangle. The red ensures that you'll stand out in a sea of black suits (or khaki pants if you're in the internet business), but the tailoring and pearls keep it classy and in control. If you're anti-red, it's OK to play it safe in black, tan or navy. The key thing to remember is to keep a conservative shape and length to the dress with a three-inch closed-toe pump. For an idea of what we're talking about, Google images of Facebook exec Sheryl Sandberg.

EASY AS 1, 2, 3

1. Sheath dress + blazer + classic jewelry

2. Camel trousers + silk blouse + slingbacks

3. Navy suit + printed blouse + classic pumps

HOW TO WEAR . . .
Florals to Work, without Looking Like a Stepford Wife

Keep it fresh, not fifties, by limiting floral prints at work to tailored pieces that look just as organized as you are. Try darker hues instead of incredibly bright ones that are more appropriate for, say, garden parties, and keep the prints simple and classic with traditional silhouettes that are neat and trim, like shirt dresses, safari dresses and shift or sheath dresses. We're big believers that a belt can make all the difference, so try adding one at your waist in a contrasting style (whether edgy, distressed or double-wrap), so the ensemble looks smart, not sticky-sweet. If it's cold, complete the look by layering a long cardigan over it and pairing it with tights, pumps or booties.

CASUAL FRIDAY

TGIF: It's the day where you can let a little bit of your personality shine—but not all of it. We do not recommend showing up at the office in full beach attire, and then chatting on the phone with your girlfriends about your upcoming trip. (We've seen it happen!) Remember, it's still a workday. To make your denim a little bit more nine-to-five, make sure the wash is super-dark, and use your accessories to dress it up. A luxe cardigan or jacket, a tucked-in shell, a skinny belt and colorful shoes keep the rest of the look so polished that it won't even seem as if you're wearing jeans at all.

EASY AS
1, 2, 3

1. White jeans **+** striped top **+** wedges
2. Dark denim trousers **+** floral top **+** khaki blazer
3. Dark skinny jeans **+** long, belted cardigan **+** flat leather boots

A FIRST DATE

First dates are nerve-racking enough as it is without having to worry about what to wear. The first rule is to choose something you're comfortable in—but not couch potato–style. Think about what you'd wear out on the town with your girlfriends and then tone it down a little. Keep comfort in mind and you'll be golden: high heels that you can actually walk in (this is where wedges become a godsend) and a handbag that seems low-maintenance, even if you're not (in other words, functional but cute bags like cross-body bags). Unless you know your first date is going to be at a skating rink or apple picking (see pages 83 and 167 for those, respectively), wearing a dress is the best course. Try a jersey dress with short or long sleeves, depending on the weather, plus a belt and a pair of wedges or high-heeled pumps that give off an effortlessly cool vibe without being too much. A day-to-night look we love, which is great for spring or summer, is to tuck

EASY AS
1, 2, 3

1. Tank **+** floral A-line skirt **+** heels
2. Nude chiffon skirt **+** leather jacket **+** booties
3. Boatneck dress (always flattering) **+** heels **+** clutch

- - - - - - - - - - - -

Harem pants

Printed cutout plat-
form wedges

Maxi-skirts

Jumpsuits, rompers

Empire-waist tops or
dresses

an everyday casual tank into a floral A-line skirt with a pair of heels or flats, which strikes just the right balance between daytime and dressy. Overall, don't confuse the guy with too many patterns, a huge handbag you have to dig through or heels so crippling you can't even walk on the sidewalk without holding onto him. Save those for the third date, at least!

A BILLIONTH DATE YOU WANT TO MAKE *FEEL* LIKE A FIRST DATE

If you're in a style rut, don't let it carry through to your relationship. A little panache can go a long way—whether you've been dating for several months or years, sometimes you just need to spice things up. Think about how you normally dress for dates—or have you resorted to wearing jeans every night?—and do some tweaking. If you tend to lean toward black dresses all the time, try a punchy color you don't normally go for or a trendy (but not overwhelming) new print, like tribal prints or watercolors. If you always wear dresses, wear your hottest pair of skinny jeans with your favorite heels, a sparkly top and a new shade of lipstick. It's not about role-playing, just keeping your guy on his toes. If you've been wearing ballet flats every Saturday night, ditch 'em for your strappiest pair of shoes, and wear your hair a little differently—put

**NO-FAIL CLOTHES
EVERY GUY LIKES**

- - - - - - - - - - - -

High heels

Tight jeans

Over-the-knee boots

V-necks

Sundresses

Mini-skirts

EASYAS
1, 2, 3

1. Strappy sandals
+ skinny jeans +
sparkly top

2. Bandage dress +
sparkly earrings +
red lipstick

3. Cutout dress +
booties + piled-on
bangles

it up in a bun and wear lots of eye makeup if you tend to wear your hair down all the time, or part it on the other side. A little change can go a long way—and it's guaranteed to make it feel like the first date all over again. But a lot less awkward. And you're sure to get that kiss at the end of the night.

EASY AS
1, 2, 3

1. Little black mini-dress + heels + layered necklaces
2. Your best-fitting jeans + killer heels + leather jacket
3. Colored or black jeans + chambray shirt + blazer

RUNNING INTO YOUR EX AT AN EVENT

So your big, bad ex is going to be at your mutual friend's party and you'll be forced to see him. This is one of the most stressful situations—especially if you're the one who got dumped. The key is to feel confident in whatever you're wearing. Obviously, you don't want the toxic bachelor back, so you want to look put together and sexy but not desperate. For this situation we like the little black mini-dress that hits midthigh with either a low-cut (but not showing too much cleavage) or off-the-shoulder neckline. Pair the dress with a killer pair of heels and you're sure to meet someone even better while working the room.

What to Wear on Date Night When You're Pregnant

Just because your bump is growing bigger by the day doesn't mean you should sit at home knitting minuscule booties in your PJs every night. Enjoy date night and look hot while you're at it by embracing your new silhouette. Luckily, maternity wear has come a long way since the muumuu movement. So show off your bump with confidence with stretchy fabrics to accommodate your growing belly and at the same time conforming to your figure. Our momfinds.com editor swears by Isabella Oliver for sexy maternity dresses. If you can't live without prints, go modern and sleek. Prints by Diane von Furstenberg are the type we're thinking—not babyish prints, as we've seen on some maternity wear. There will be plenty of time for those—on your little one.

AS A TOURIST,
WITHOUT LOOKING LIKE ONE

Congrats—you've finally done it—requested a few days off from work, booked a flight and maybe you've even downloaded a French language DVD to your iPhone to prepare. No matter where you're headed, whether it's NYC, the Caribbean or a European jaunt, nobody wants to look like a tourist. We once interviewed British designer Lulu Guinness about this very predicament, since she's known for traveling back and forth from the States to the UK. Her advice? If you're heading for a city, ban the

khaki from your wardrobe and opt for black. Same goes for white running shoes—they're a dead giveaway. Need we mention the fanny packs? We honestly hope not—they are wrong for so many reasons.

You don't need a tourist uniform to go sightseeing—you just need to feel comfortable. Bring along those jersey dresses, your most comfortable sandals (don't even try to wear them with socks!) and a streamlined handbag with lots of interior pockets. Lulu says if you're heading to Europe, use the opportunity to wear your more flamboyant pieces at night, whether that means your sequin jacket or satin pants that have been sitting in your closet for eons. (Europeans in general tend to be somewhat more daring, fashion-wise, than Americans.) If you're heading on a beach vacay, lucky girl, leave the black at home in favor of lightweight whites, linens, a cool summer hat and, of course, an amazing pair of sunglasses. Swap the trainers for TOMS or Bensimons, which even Brigitte Bardot used to wear, a pair of moccasins or desert boots. Can't argue with that, huh? Bring along more than one swimsuit to keep things interesting, and definitely bring a bunch of chunky jewelry to make your outfits feel fresh, without having to buy an entirely new wardrobe.

EASY AS
1, 2, 3

1. Jersey dress **+** flat sandals **+** denim jacket
2. Structured printed tank **+** white jeans **+** ballet flats
3. Dark denim **+** jewel-toned cardigans or cropped jacket **+** Bensimon shoes

WHILE SHOPPING FOR MORE THINGS TO WEAR

It may seem counterintuitive: Why should you care about what you're wearing while looking for more clothes? In reality, what you wear while shopping will absolutely determine what you end up buying. If you wear something shlubby, you're going to end up spending way too much money on clothes. (We have both made this mistake before!) Do your laundry before you go shopping so you know what you have. Running out of underwear? Add it to your list. Can't find a decent white T-shirt or pair of jeans that haven't shrunk? Have no work dresses that are in style? You know what to do. Now, put on something you actually like to wear. Your favorite outfit is best. We prefer shopping in dresses and flats, whether that means flat boots, sandals or ballet flats, because you can get around more easily, and you can slip your dress on and off in lots of dressing rooms. So choose a loose-fitting, flattering dress you can take off easily (preferably by pulling it over your head—lots of buttons misses the point). If you're shopping for a dress for a specific occasion, bring the shoes you'll be wearing with it along with you in your bag so there's no guesswork involved. It will change the way you shop, guaranteed.

EASY AS

1, 2, 3

1. Jersey dress **+** trench coat **+** flats
2. V-neck tee **+** leggings **+** leather jacket
3. Jumpsuit **+** sandals **+** anorak

AT THE DOG PARK

Two things to keep in mind when taking the dog out for a playdate: You're probably going to get dirty and you'll need to be able to pick up the poop. The dog park is a very social place and you never know who you might meet. Your next boss or boyfriend could be filling up the water bowl, so this is not the place where you want to completely slob it out. Dark jeans are a good choice because pawprints can be dusted off—just make sure they're midrise. You don't want to flash your underwear to the crowd (canine and human). Slim-cut T-shirts or merino wool sweaters work on top. In the fall we love the look of a trim leather jacket and a bright pashmina scarf. Good shoes are essential. A pair of ballet flats, TOMS slip-ons or stylish sneakers are the way to go. If it's wet or snowing, break out the Hunter boots. No heels allowed—you'll sink into the dirt, mud and grass. If you must have some elevation (we're giving a shout-out to all our petite friends here—you know who you are), we approve of platform-wedge espadrilles. Keep the color dark and the material durable. We once saw a guy in crested velvet house slippers in the run—he stood in the corner the entire time, terrified of getting his shoes dirty.

EASY AS
1, 2, 3

1. Leather jacket + tank + dark skinny jeans
2. Trench + bright scarf + leggings
3. Chambray top + colorful jeans or shorts + layering tank

ON THE COMMUTE, UNTIL YOU MAKE IT BIG AND CAN HIRE A DRIVER, OF COURSE

EASYAS

1, 2, 3

1. Trench **+** rain boots **+** chunky knit cap

2. Wool ¾ length coat **+** beret **+** elbow-length gloves

3. Olive army coat **+** faux fur vest **+** knit gloves

We're big proponents of leaving your heels at work. It might sound funny, but your commute will be a million times better if you can actually walk to and from public transportation or the parking lot pain-free. So now that we've got that down pat, make sure your commuting shoes are sturdy and well-made. Get a great pair of flat leather boots, a pair of ballet flats or oxfords that stay on your feet and a flat pair of sandals for summer. If it rains a lot in your region, it won't hurt to invest in stylish rain boots (in other words, no duckies allowed—see page 95). Your work wardrobe is up to you, but outerwear is important. A trench coat that fits well, with a belt to tie around, and a winter coat that's thick and warm and in a neutral color, with gloves, scarves and thick socks for layering in cold weather, are your best bests. Don't put a bunch of random stuff together—think about how it all looks together as a package. If you wouldn't mind your boss seeing you in your newfound commuting outfits, you're good to go. Go forth and conquer.

HOSTING A PARTY AT HOME, WITHOUT LOOKING LIKE YOU'RE TRYING TOO HARD

You've sent the Evites out, and even gotten your friends to RSVP (a feat in itself). You've planned the menu, ordered the booze—you're almost there. Don't be one of those hosts who is flitting around moments before the party, unshowered, and unsure of what you're wearing. If you're cooking today, make sure that, first and foremost, whatever you're wearing is not going to catch on fire—in other words, no bell sleeves or flammable materials. Wear something versatile enough for all the last-minute hostess duties.

Consider a long, printed maxi-dress or a chic jumpsuit—nothing says "host" better than a dramatic entrance. A word to the wise: Wear something printed or dark in color—the better to hide the inevitable stains that are bound to find their way onto your ensemble. As the host, you'll be all over the place, so choose a pair of cute shoes that are also comfortable—you're signing up for a lot of running around. If the party's casual, consider a pair of dark jeans, a sassy black V-neck top and a cropped satin jacket for extra drama. Pile on the jewelry—it's your time to shine.

EASY AS
1, 2, 3

1. Maxi-dress + cardigan + earrings
2. Jumpsuit + booties + bangles
3. Dark jeans + V-neck top + cropped satin or tweed jacket

AT THE LADIES' LUNCHEON

We do a lot of networking in our business and more often than not we are invited to dine on poached chicken salads while exchanging business cards. If you want to make an impression, you've got to wear something that will get you noticed in a tasteful way. Most people will be wearing black dresses or pantsuits. Stand out in a tailored sheath dress—we like pink or red—or a Diane von Furstenberg wrap dress, known for eye-catching prints. Another good way to get women interested in chatting with you is to wear an amazing statement necklace—like a long strand of turquoise stones—or carry a brightly colored "It" bag. This makes it easy for people to approach you because they can open with "I love your bag/necklace/dress." Sounds petty, but it's true!

EASY AS
1, 2, 3

1. Purple long-sleeved dress **+** gray suede shoes **+** cocktail ring
2. Printed wrap dress **+** tailored blazer **+** statement necklace
3. Colorful cropped jacket **+** monochromatic skirt **+** tights

MEETING THE FUTURE IN-LAWS

One of the more stress-inducing situations a woman can go through: dining with the boyfriend's parental units. Ben Stiller made the practice famous: Now it's your turn to meet the parents. The first time meeting them is always a bit hazardous. You'll be overdoing it if you appear ultraconservative and they might think you're weird if you break out the super-eclectic, trendy stuff. Overdo it on the cleavage-inducing tops, mini-skirts or tight

EASY AS
1, 2, 3

1. Denim trouser jeans **+** silk floral top **+** lightweight cardigan

2. Sheath dress **+** statement necklace **+** wedges (or other sensible heels)

3. A-line skirt **+** denim jacket **+** scoop-neck tee

jeans and you risk looking like you're not worth Junior's time. When you're having your own Kate Middleton moment (we're looking at you, navy Issa dress), it's best to choose something in a solid color, with a modest silhouette, like a sheath dress or a pair of wide-leg black pants with a crisp, classic button-down sweater. A scoop neck keeps everything PG. If it's a spring brunch and therefore not too formal, stay casual with neutral-colored sandals. Just make sure to leave the beat-up beach thongs at home. Let your flair show through in your accessories. Break out an extra-long necklace or a chunky embellished cuff to spice up the neutral color palette. Finally, a bold red handbag will show the 'rents that you don't take yourself too seriously.

STAYING AT YOUR IN-LAWS' OVERNIGHT

Say you go to visit your in-laws and you're obligated to wake up at the crack of dawn because Mom is making her famous French toast and your husband insists you don't dress up for breakfast. "Just roll out of bed and come to the table," he says. Your husband's ratty old college T-shirt and a pair of boxer shorts aren't going to cut it. So what's a girl to wear when lounging with her guy's family? We suggest ditching the shorts for a pair of cashmere yoga pants in a jersey gray. The material keeps it luxe while the color downplays the ensemble. On top, opt for a simple cotton tank in a solid, darker color so your bra (yes, you have to wear a bra to breakfast) doesn't show through. Look for a tank that's long in length so your midriff won't peek out. If you're of the modest camp (or, more important, your in-laws are), cover up with a button-down boyfriend cardigan in basic black. It'd be wise not to prance around in your bare feet unless the rules of the house call for you to do so. Slip on a pair of slippers (satin ballet flats work here, too) before heading to the table, and make sure your unruly bedhead is somewhat tamed. A simple headband and a run-through with the brush, and a swipe of blush, will do the trick.

EASYAS
1, 2, 3

1. Cashmere yoga pants **+** V-neck tee **+** cardigan
2. Leggings **+** long-sleeved henley **+** slippers
3. Cotton-linen pants **+** striped tank **+** zip-up sweater

YOUR BOSS'S COCKTAIL PARTY THAT'S ALLEGEDLY NOT A WORK EVENT

EASYAS
1, 2, 3

1. Sleeveless white blouse **+** printed skirt **+** cardigan

2. Little black dress **+** suede heels **+** neutral clutch

3. Navy shift dress **+** sandals **+** oversized clutch

While seeing your boss on the off-hours might not be your first choice of how to spend a weekend, it's part of your duty as an employee. So opt for understated chic: You can never go wrong with black, and form-fitting dresses and skirts are the ideal way to go. A simple black cocktail dress (which, by the way, you should already have if you've been following our advice), plus some great jewelry, black suede heels you can walk in and a neutral clutch will do the trick. Don't go overboard—and definitely don't have too many drinks. Make the rounds, sample the finger food and enjoy yourself—while paying compliments to the host, er, boss, of course. Don't forget the thank-you note, either. If the party is in the spring or summer, swap your black for navy and add some color with a clutch in an exotic skin or contrasting hues like yellow, coral or green. Absolutely make sure you've got a pedicure if you're wearing sandals, and if it's a casual outdoor party, try a mix of fun and conservative, like a sleeveless white blouse, a long, chunky chain-link necklace, a printed skirt and a dark denim jacket or neutral cardigan.

PULLING OFF THE UBIQUITOUS DAY-TO-NIGHT SWITCH

It's the transition everyone's always talking about—how do you make that crucial after-work transition from chic worker bee to cute girl at happy hour without looking like a harlot at your desk and like a librarian at the bar? And, sorry, but who has all the time in the world to rush all the way home to shower and change? It's all in the accessories, baby, which we suggest you stash in a clutch under your desk for quick changes. First, you'll need some basic transitional pieces. A blazer, for instance, is a magical piece as far as we're concerned. It's all business, and easy to just shed and shove in your bag on the way out your office door. Blazers are for beginners: If you have a black one for winter, get another, lightweight one in a lighter color for summer days. It'll also keep you feeling comfortable in corporate air-conditioning. Whether you work in a creative atmosphere, or if you're entrenched in an extremely corporate work environment, a blazer will work whether paired with some well-fitting jeans or black pants, or even a

THINGS TO STASH IN YOUR DESK DRAWER
- - - - - - - - - - - - -
1. A pair of sexy heels
2. A collar necklace
3. A metallic clutch

silky club-appropriate halter. (Voilà. If you're not a fan of blazers, a cropped black jacket with a satin or leather collar works well, too.)

Now onto jewelry. Before you buy anything, scour your jewelry collection for fun necklaces, cocktail rings, earrings and cuffs. We like big, chunky, attention-getting pieces—the kind that garner all the compliments when you wear them—or lots of delicate jewelry layered. The more eclectic the better. After all, most people on any given day only see you from the

chest up (at your desk, bar or restaurant), so go for a flattering neckline and some eye-catching jewelry in a pinch. Shoes are less important in this day-to-night kind of dressing, but, of course, it doesn't hurt to throw into the mix a great pair of heels that are higher and sexier than your work pumps. If you're the trouser type, you can change into a pair of jeans; if you're into dresses, wear a simple form-fitting sheath with a jacket to work, then take the jacket off and add the jewelry. With just these few pieces, you'll find that you can do the day-to-night transition like a pro.

As for handbags, store a big envelope clutch in your office and just bring along the essentials. Nothing kills a buzz more than heading to margarita night with a briefcase. If you're headed out of town on a Friday, here are some weekend tips. For spring and summer, buy sundresses that can double as play clothes—for a park picnic, ballgame or garden party—and wear them with flat sandals or wedges during the day, then add your jewelry and heels for night. Slick on some bronzer, brush your hair out and you're ready to go. If it's fall or winter, black pants or jeans paired with flat boots with cardigans are daytime-perfect for catching flights, running errands, going to movies and apple picking—then change into heeled boots, jewelry, swap the cardigan for a leather jacket and you're all set to take the night by storm.

CHAPTER 9

What to Wear to All Those Friggin' Weddings

As a guest to a wedding, you have a responsibility to show up in the right attire. This is not the time to wear whatever you want—take into consideration the time of day the wedding will take place (an afternoon garden setting is much more subdued than an evening wedding in a ballroom) and any dress code specifications. Remember, there will be a professional photographer there (plus lots of Facebook photos, for all of eternity), so put your best foot forward.

The Rules: Wedding Edition

A few basic wedding rules we've picked up along the way:

✦ *Never* wear white and you might as well steer clear of ivory, too (unless you are the bride).

✦ Don't wear black to a Southern wedding.

✦ Steer clear of red, which is considered gauche in some circles.

✦ Ditto for animal prints (unless you're going for the cougar look).

✦ Don't show too much skin (you don't want Grandma asking, "Who invited the hussy?").

Since each wedding is different, we've rounded up your best looks for every wedding imaginable (from the preppy golf course soiree to the strict Orthodox gathering) so you can fit in and feel your best as you toast the happy couple, no matter what the invitation says.

Your No-Fail Shopping List

Five items to buy so you will *always* have something to wear to a wedding:

1 A sleeveless, knee-length black dress in tropical-weight wool.

2 A light-colored, knee-length sheath dress in silk or tropical-weight wool.

3 A solid neutral-color shawl or shrug if you need to cover up due to weather or church rules.

4 Open-toe black strappy sandals.

5 Closed-toe nude pumps.

THE SEMIFORMAL WEDDING

HOW TO SPOT IT

A wedding that starts after 5 p.m. usually calls for at least semiformal dress. The invitation will be less formal than a black-tie wedding invitation (see page 233), both in overall look and in the language used.

WHAT TO WEAR

Most weddings fall into the semiformal category, which basically means that people will show up in everything from cotton sundresses to little black cocktail dresses. We think that a wedding after sunset is the perfect excuse to play dress-up and tend to lean toward breaking out a party dress. We like to wear color to a wedding to stand out from the black and white lineup at the altar. There's no reason you have to dress in drab colors—you just can't look slutty, so no super-plunging wild necklines. As a fabulous friend of ours says, "Let your aisle be my runway!" Try a knee-length dress in a color that looks fab on you—be it cobalt, turquoise or tangerine. Silk, satin or heavy cotton are all fine—just stay away from taffeta lest you look like a runaway bridesmaid.

THE COUNTRY CLUB WEDDING

HOW TO SPOT IT

Muffy and Winston attended prep school together and met on the polo team? You're in for a preppy wedding with all the trimmings. You may even see some salmon-colored pants if you're lucky.

WHAT TO WEAR

Even if you've never set foot in a country club, now is not the time to experiment with new trends. If the wedding is during the day, stick to a floral or pastel look. If you're not comfortable in floral, go full-on Lilly Pulitzer. There's no need to look like a

Stepford wife—a simple sheath dress or tea-length A-line dress that flatters your figure will do. As for the shoes, opt for a pair of low heels, because nothing is more garish at a prepster's wedding than edgy YSL pumps that will poke holes in that award-winning golf course.

THE CASUAL DAYTIME WEDDING

HOW TO SPOT IT
No bridezillas here. The invite is cheeky; the wording on it nontraditional. Your two spunkiest friends ask you to come watch them get hitched in their backyard—maybe it's a no-frills couple or a second marriage—but the dress is "casual."

WHAT TO WEAR
No matter how low-maintenance your friends are, please don't show up in Tevas or a pair of running sneakers (we've actually seen this happen, and it was a disaster). It's still a wedding, so go for something bright and festive, like a punchy-colored A-line dress or a floral sheath cinched with a smart belt and a pair of wedges, or a pencil skirt with a silk camisole or a button-down shirt and a cardigan. A smart pantsuit will work, too—just make sure it fits you well—and wear a bright silk tank underneath so you don't look all-business.

THE BLACK-TIE AFFAIR

HOW TO SPOT IT

Invitations for formal weddings will typically be spelled out. If you don't see *Black Tie* written on the invitation itself, do a little detective work: Is the font a large, curly script, written on heavy card stock? That's a more subtle tip-off that you're expected to dress to the nines.

WHAT TO WEAR

This is not the time to resurrect your cheapie summer dress from the closet. Invest in a black strapless or short-sleeved gown in a luxurious fabric like satin or chiffon. Gloves are optional, but bring along a fun bejeweled or metallic clutch to stash them in if you intend to grab an hors d'oeuvre or two. Contrary to what you may see at black-tie galas portrayed in movies, leave the tiara at home, please.

WHAT DOES *BLACK TIE OPTIONAL* REALLY MEAN?

– – – – – – – – – – – –

Q: The invitation to my friend's wedding says "black tie optional." What does that mean? I don't want to offend anyone.

A: The bride and groom are simply giving their guests the choice, to dress up in black tie attire or wear something cocktail-worthy. A general rule is to make sure your fabrics look luxe and that you accessorize tastefully, but no need to break out the ball gown, unless you opt to!

THE JUSTICE OF THE PEACE CEREMONY

HOW TO SPOT IT

Your no-frills, workaholic coworker sends you an email at lunch inviting you to her reception after work. Just a simple trip to the courthouse will do for this lady, followed by happy-hour drinks with the accounting team.

WHAT TO WEAR

If the low-key bride is donning the cream-colored suit she wore to work, don't outshine her in the cocktail dress you have stashed in your filing cabinet for unexpected events. Stick with a neutral sheath (no loud patterns) and a pair of slingbacks with a low heel. Keep it simple and nobody gets hurt.

THE DESTINATION
BEACHFRONT BLOWOUT

HOW TO SPOT IT

The invite arrives two years before the date—you've got to book a flight, a hotel room, a rental car and alert the bride of any allergies to shellfish for the seaside clambake.

WHAT TO WEAR

Leave the swimsuit and flip-flops in your suitcase. For the ceremony and reception, opt for a long, printed maxi-dress, which was made for exotic locales. Just make sure it's not too long, or you'll trip on the dance floor later. Since you've spent your savings on a plane ticket, skip the shoe splurge and slip into a pair of strappy flat sandals. No one will see them anyway. Make sure to bring a wrap—those ocean breezes can get chilly.

THE ORTHODOX WEDDING

HOW TO SPOT IT

If the ceremony takes place in a place of worship, look carefully at the name of the church, mosque, temple or synagogue, and go a step further to see if it has a website. This little bit of research may help you dress appropriately. If all the members are photographed wearing hats in the photos, you'll be one step ahead. If the church has *Orthodox* in its name, the dress code will most likely be even more conservative. Obtaining this information will prevent embarrassment/strange looks/banishment later.

WHAT TO WEAR

It's considered disrespectful to show too much skin or draw too much attention to yourself in these places of worship, so find a jacket, cardigan or blazer to cover up your bare shoulders, or wear a dress with three-quarter-length sleeves. Cleavage and exposed skin have no place here—even if it's ninety degrees and humid, this still holds true. You want the officiant to be focused on the couple, not on your chest, so chose a tasteful shift dress in a muted color or a rounded neckline that extends up to the collarbone. Same goes for hemlines—make sure your dress hemline hits at the knee or below. If tea-length dresses work for your shape, meaning you don't have wide calves, wear one here. Get yourself a great pair of pumps. Nothing over three inches, though. Not to worry: Your feet will thank you on the dance floor. In many of these places, bare legs are sinful, so wear (or bring) a pair of pantyhose. If the reception afterwards is less buttoned-up, you can always remove them, along with your jacket, later.

{ CHAPTER 10 }

Jet-Setting Style
WHAT TO WEAR ON THOSE GETAWAYS

That's it: Your tickets are booked to a city you've never been to before—now how to decide what to pack? The chic traveler fits in as a local and doesn't scream *tourist*. You also don't want to show up dressed in NYC black when everyone else is in Palm Springs turquoise. Looking like a local is especially important to get good service at local spots.

A good way to figure out what the locals consider cool is to ask friends you know in the area. Another option if you're really serious about fitting in is to look at regional magazine websites to get a feel for what's in fashion. The party shots of the glitterati and influential on these sites will show you what's cool and hip in your destination and what's appropriate colorwise and how formal you need to be after the sun sets. In the United States there are mainly two publishers of these type of magazines: Find a full list of the cities they cover at NicheMediaLLC.com and ModernLuxury.com.

With these helpful tips you'll always be in style, no matter what the destination. Be sure to bring along your passport, your sense of adventure and your camera—and bon voyage!

LUGGAGE

Smart women don't check bags. If you pack wisely you should be able to put everything into a wheeled carry-on. A few musts for luggage:

1. It should be strong. Luggage is not the place to go for fashion brands. You want strength, not cuteness, and unfortunately luggage with celebrities' names on it is not the most durable. Samsonite and Tumi are our two go-to brands for bags that won't break down on you in the middle of a run to the gate.

2. It must fit in the overhead bin. Get a gate agent or flight attendant who is in a foul mood and, if your bag is a teensy bit tough to stuff into the overhead, she'll toss it right off the plane. At the rate the airlines lose luggage you definitely don't want to be _that_ person who has to restock a week's worth of clothing at the local Gap. To play it safe don't buy a suitcase larger than 22" × 14" × 9". Any bigger and you're playing roulette when you walk down that gangway.

FOUR ITEMS TO PACK FOR WHEREVER YOU'RE GOING

- - - - - - - - - - - - -

1. Sunglasses

2. A brightly colored shawl or wrap

3. Black jeans

4. Black flats

3. Pay attention to weight. You can't rely on the cute guy in 24C to help you hoist your bag into the overhead, so you want your bag to be as light as possible when empty. The range can be from four to ten pounds for the same size bag, so make sure you check those specs on the product detail before you click to buy.

4. Opt for wheels. It feels like the hike from the curb to gate just keeps getting longer and longer so give your spine a break and make sure you have wheels on your bag. Look for "spinner" wheels—four multi-directional wheels that mean your luggage will make quick turns with you without falling over or slowing you down.

5. Add a bit of flare. Since we don't recommend fashion luggage, you're going to need to do something to your bag to make it stand out from others. We've heard horror stories of ladies opening a bag for a romantic weekend to find it full of some guy's boxer briefs. To distinguish your bag, tie a pretty grosgrain ribbon to the handle, wrap a bright belt around your bag and get a distinctive hang tag. Luglife.com is a great site to shop for tags and cords in cool designs.

TIP
- - - - - - - - - - - -
Luggage is a great item to buy online because you can get the model number off any website and then search across the web for the best deal. Start at luggage.com and ebags.com to get the scoop on reviews and features, and then cast your net wide on Google to get the best price.

HOW TO DRESS TO GET
BUMPED INTO FIRST CLASS

It's astounding how sloppily people dress now when they fly. It's as if some of these people don't realize they're in public in an airport. Not only are they in public, but they are in close proximity to absolute strangers.

Some essential rules for plane travel: You absolutely may not wear tank tops (unless as a layering piece under something else), flip-flops, mini-skirts, sweats, crop tops—nothing that will expose your skin to the herd that's flying with you. Don't even

think about wearing pajamas—it's not appropriate unless you're under the age of five. Now if you want to take it up a notch and try to score an upgrade, the key is to look quiet and respectable. Upgrades are rare and it's frequently up to the discretion of the gate agent. Wear dark business casual or business apparel. A neutral blazer, dark top and black or gray wool pants with low-heel pumps give you your best shot.

SKY-HIGH COMFORT: HOW TO LOOK GREAT AND FLY RIGHT

We pack only a carry-on, do check-ins online, flit through security—shoes already in hand—and spend our (minimal) waiting time briskly walking the terminal, because we'll be sitting enough on the plane. The most fundamental flight factor, though, is your outfit. Well-chosen clothing can make the difference between a cold, painful trip and a comfortable, restful one.

Light dress: The freedom of a dress allows you to curl, cross or stretch your legs without restriction, and to shift endlessly in your seat without exposing your belly or back. When you get off the plane, you'll be street-ready—because do you really want to waste precious sake-sipping or Palermo-shopping time changing from your "travel clothes"? To really hit the ground running, choose travel-friendly fabrics like cotton-nylon blends, jersey knits or cashmere—these materials are all lightweight and wrinkle-resistant.

Shoes: The need for foot coverage means you can't wear sandals, so think in terms of low-heeled shoes or flats. They're essential when you're racing through Terminal 5 to catch that departing plane—just make sure they're easy to remove (and put back on) when you get to security. Tory Burch ballet flats are modern classics that will slide on and off quickly.

Supportive cami: Like beauty, comfort comes from the inside out: Don't forget to tweak the most elementary aspect of your outfit. A shaping camisole, like Jockey's 3-D Seamless camisole, won't ever pinch or poke, and its silky texture feels great against the skin—even for ten or twelve hours at a time.

Don't forget a **lightweight scarf** for extra layers to keep you warm. And when the plane pillows are scarce, you can roll this one up and use it to rest your weary head.

You also want a **large tote bag** in which you can stuff magazines, laptops and anything else you'll need while out of town. We never check bags so this is the way to get as much stuff as possible on the plane without having to gate-check.

Celebrity Airport Style: What We've Learned from the Tabloids

Take your style cues from the A-listers—as professional travelers with a trail of paparazzi everywhere, they know what they're doing and how to always look good.

✦ **Pack a hat.** Hair can get flat after a long flight. Everybody on the ground doesn't need to see that you've got bedhead. Try chunky knits in winter and straw versions in summer.

✦ **Keep makeup in your carry-on.** For easy access, toss your gloss, concealer, bronzer and mascara in your bag so you can freshen up after the flight. Bonus: If you lose your luggage, at least you'll look somewhat pulled together.

✦ **Bring flip-flops** to change into on the plane for a way to get to the bathroom without putting the shoes back on or going in your socks.

OUTFIT IN A PINCH: TAKING A PRIVATE JET

– – – – – – – – – – – –

Look who's rubbing elbows with the "in" crowd. Dress simply and elegantly for your first ride in a private jet. If you wear Juicy Couture sweatpants, you'll never, ever get invited back. Try a navy or neutral shift dress; printed pink, navy and white scarf; a white linen blazer; oversized sunglasses and a colorful pair of sandals. Bring along a smart leather tote bag, and you're off.

Send us a postcard!

U.S. ROAD TRIP

It's been your dream to drive cross-country with your best girlfriends, and now it's finally coming true. Be strategic about what you bring with you. Most likely, you won't have a ton of room in the car, so bring only the pieces you really feel comfortable in—after all, you're going to be in the car for so many hours, the last thing you need is a wardrobe meltdown. Bring pieces that can work double duty, like a tunic, white jeans and sandals that can easily take you from the car to the beach at a moment's notice.

A large tote will come in handy for souvenirs and quick jaunts through towns. Don't bother bringing jewelry with you—pick some up at the hundreds of cool vintage shops waiting for you to discover them. Bring a towel or two, a great pair of UV-protected sunglasses and layers. You might want to consider leggings for the car ride— the more lightweight the better so you can wash them at a rest stop and let them dry overnight. Your legs will get cold from sitting right next to the A/C otherwise. Don't forget to bring a few dresses in case you come across some amazing restaurants you want to try—it would be a shame to be turned away just because of the dress code. After all, you may never be back. Most important, check the weather—if the East Coast is expecting a heat wave or a cold front, you should be prepared so you don't have to make unnecessary stops along the way.

EAST COAST: HAMPTONS, CAPE COD, NEWPORT

These summer beach destinations are just as much about status as the gorgeous beachfront views from the old-school mansions. Dress the part in all-American separates. Stripes and geometric prints, paired with solids, will be your best friends here. Try striped tanks, jackets, seersucker skirts or wedge sandals—just not all at once, of course. Cropped linen pants will look chic and tailored during the chilly nights with a chunky sweater. Plus—don't forget it— a lightweight anorak should it rain.

For lounging, a simple white button-down tunic and a pair of madras will make you look like you fit right in. Safari dresses and sundresses are appropriate both during the day and at night— bring a belt or two to accessorize. Brown or metallic accents will add contrast. If you're attending a dressier affair, a crisp pair of high-waist sailor jeans and a flowy, tucked-in blouse are timeless.

Bring along some platform sandals, the better to balance out the flowy, flowery pieces. A great canvas tote—invaluable for those trips to the market for corn and lobsters—doubles as a beach bag. Go for solid, bold bikinis or one-pieces on the beach—reds, navys, kelly green, even black are great choices, and they look chic with an oversized floppy straw hat and round or oval sunglasses.

WEST COAST: NAPA VALLEY, SAN FRANCISCO, CATALINA

Many out-of-towners make the mistake of thinking that just because it's California, it's hot outside all year round. If you're going to these parts during summer, it can get as cold as forty-five degrees in the evening. Pack appropriately. White jeans, skinny cargo pants, safari jackets, lightweight scarves and jersey cardigans will all come in handy. Mix them with lighter tanks and V-neck tees, and don't forget to add some fun jewelry. Throw in tie-dye, stone jewelry or fringe—this is the West Coast, so anything goes. A pair of funky closed-toe espadrilles will fight off a chill while still looking season-appropriate.

Maxi-dresses were born on the West Coast: Bring a few of these along and you'll fit right in. Note: In San Francisco specifically, a 4 p.m. chill encroaches on the city, so try an A-line skirt with a belted anorak, scarf and wedges. A boho blouse plus dark trouser jeans and sunglasses are great for chillier days, too.

EXOTIC BEACH VACATIONS, FROM BALI TO HAWAII

It's all about the prints in vibrant corals, navys and yellows. Make sure you've got several tunics in all kinds of prints, one for each day of the week, with a pair of gorgeous sandals with a fringe or some other kind of embellishment. Let your bikini speak for itself—loud prints in a flattering cut. And why not do as the models on runways do and pile on a handmade necklace with your bikini? It's pretty chic if you ask us. Brocade shorts, organic cotton burnout tees and big hearty jeweled cuffs and coral necklaces will make your everyday pieces seem super-exotic.

DOING EUROPE

Go for minimalism in edgy chic neutrals paired with metallics. We love the look of khaki dresses with metallic sandals, black, red or white pants with sequin tees, blazers and high-heeled sandals, plus exotic totes, and cutout maillots instead of the traditional bikini. At the beach, wear a large, black floppy hat—the epitome of chic—and some ivory cuffs. Black and white are also at home here—you'll blend right in, from city to cabana. At night, you've got to dress up—that's what really separates the natives from the tourists.

Put your hair up in a bun, add a shot of red lipstick, a classic little black dress, lace sheath or red one-shoulder number, and you'll have those European men eating out of the palm of your hand.

EXPLORING AFRICA

Whether you're jetting off to Morocco to enjoy the couscous and troll the bazaars or you're poolside at your luxe hotel in Marrakesh, these outfits will be perfect for your trip.

Serious bargains work better in separates: Go for a cropped cap-sleeve top, a pair of silk harem pants and jeweled flats. Pair these with tribal earrings for a luxe look. Try a silk and cotton tunic in a gorgeous color, a jeweled linen clutch and embellished mirrored flats. Poolside, don't forget your sunglasses, a barely there bikini and a straw beach tote.

CHAPTER 11

Super Special Occasions
WHAT TO WEAR
DURING YOUR MILESTONES

BIG BIRTHDAYS

IT'S YOUR PARTY—YOU SHOULD WEAR WHAT YOU WANT TO . . .

We believe that birthdays should be celebrated in a huge way, no matter what age you're turning, but when it comes to those really big fat birthdays that end in a zero, the ones that mark a "holy shit" beginning of a decade, you've got to step up to the fashion plate.

IF YOU'RE TURNING TWENTY, OR, ER, TWENTY-ONE, WHICH IS PROBABLY MORE OF A MILESTONE

Live it up, girl. You're finally of legal drinking age, so bottoms up. Wear something that shows off your figure in your favorite color or print. You've heard the phrase, you only live once—well, you only turn twenty-one once—after this, no birthday holds as much importance. (So what if you can't rent a car until you're twenty-five? That doesn't count.) For the rest of your life, you'll remember (or not remember, depending on how much alcohol you consume) this one the most and compare most birthdays to it, even when you're old and gray. Ours were spent stumbling around drunkenly, in dresses we adored, even though they came from big box stores like H&M and Forever21, ironically enough. All it takes is a lively spirit to make a cheap and trendy dress look cool. Cheers, birthday girl.

Dancing Queen:
Five Comfortable Shoe Brands
Made to Last All Night Long

No flip-flops or bare feet on the dance floor for us. While it's true you may not be able to afford the best at every age, here are our favorite shoe brands for dancing in—they're all seriously comfortable and sexy at the same time.

1 **Cole Haan.** Not just your boyfriend's loafers, these heels stand apart from the pack with Nike Air technology in the sole!

2 **Faryl Robin.** The chunkier heels are not only trendy, but they help with balance, too. Win-win.

3 **Stuart Weitzman.** Sometimes paying more for shoes can pay off. These are classic and oh-so-easy to walk in.

4 **Giuseppe Zannotti.** Trust us, we've seen them cut in half—there are layers and layers of padding and a ton of effort goes into meticulously manufacturing them. So worth the price.

5 **Banana Republic.** Surprising, but it's true. These babies seem to have extra shock absorbers near the ball of your foot—and you can usually find them on sale for under $100.

IF YOU'RE TURNING THIRTY

By now, you've tried every trend, from cutouts and crop tops to neons, maxi-skirts and even leather pants—and your bank statement proves it. All that experimenting has left you with an edited-down wardrobe that you can really live with. Now take all that knowledge and buy yourself a dress no one has ever seen you wear before. Does white complement your complexion better than anything else, or is red the shade that gets you in the mood to party? Whatever it is, wear it: It's your birthday. You don't need a $1,000 dress to look cool—just find something that makes you feel sexy, get a great pair of heels and you're all good. Just promise us you won't end the night searching for crow's feet and throwing pity parties like the girls in those chick flicks always tend to do on their thirtieth. Rewrite the script tonight.

EASYAS
1, 2, 3

1. Punchy party dress **+** cropped jacket **+** studded belt

2. Wide-leg pants **+** tucked-in chiffon top **+** oversized baubles

3. Colorblock sheath **+** strappy shoes **+** brocade trench

EASY AS 1, 2, 3

1. Form-fitting dress or pants in rich fabric + tailored evening jacket + cocktail ring
2. Jewel-toned blouse + skinny black pants + sky-high heels
3. Black lace sheath + dangly earrings + pumps

EASY AS 1, 2, 3

1. Backless dress + cocktail ring + red lipstick
2. Satin pants + tuxedo jacket + jeweled shoes
3. Wide-leg camel pants + silk neutral-colored tee + red strappy sandals

IF YOU'RE TURNING FORTY

If the *Real Housewives* franchise has taught us anything, it's that you don't have to curl up and die on the day of your fortieth birthday. The fun is just getting started. Whether you're going out or hosting a bash at your home, turn to your favorite designers for this special day. Show off your assets, and if you haven't gotten on the Spanx train yet, trust us, it's the best birthday present ever. Inst-abs, which is perfect for those form-fitting dresses you admire so much.

IF YOU'RE TURNING FIFTY AND BEYOND

Your birthday suit (not the one you were born with) should be all about gorgeous fabrics and gorgeous prints in colors that flatter your complexion. If you're not comfortable baring a lot of skin, consider a pair of slouchy satin pants, a bejeweled shoe and a printed shell with a cropped jacket. Be true to yourself. If you love dresses, you can still incorporate the trends into your look without looking like a minor. The key when you're in your fifties and beyond is tailoring. Make sure whatever you wear fits you impeccably: That's the difference

between you and your younger self. You're better
acquainted with your body type by now—there's
no excuse for ill-fitting clothes.

FIRST DAY OF WORK

Well, congratulations! You landed the job you've been dreaming about—and now reality sets in. You'll have to make all new office friends, learn to work with a completely different boss and adhere to an unfamiliar set of office rules. But, more important, what will you wear? It seems like the single most daunting task, like the first day of school.

With butterflies in your stomach, all of a sudden the old sheaths that worked in your last gig suddenly don't seem to fly. You're back in junior high, except this time it's not about impressing your crush: It's all about the first impression, and your career.

We can't tell you that no one is going to notice your shoes or that no one will judge you—quite the opposite. But the key is to be yourself, just an elevated version of yourself. People will be curious about you—after all, you're the new girl. So your accessories will speak for you more than you may have the chance to speak for yourself, depending on the office atmosphere. It shouldn't be completely foreign to you: You should have a sense of what the industry norms are or, at the very least, noticed what the others were wearing on your interview. A good rule of thumb is to dress more formally than you did at your previous job—kick it up a notch for the first week. Give yourself extra time in the morning to blow-dry your hair nicely. Get a new pair of shoes and ditch the scuffed ones. You want to toe the line between being approachable and gaining respect from your bosses. Let your boss and your coworkers know that your boss knew what she was doing when she hired you. Bring along a sophisticated handbag that isn't too flashy—make sure it's functional and can hold all

SNEAKY STYLING TRICK

To tuck your jeans into boots, it helps if your denim has a little bit of stretch—even just one percent will do.

WHAT TO WEAR . . .
When Your Bust Is Too Big for a Blazer

While we do love a great blazer (especially for day-to-night dressing to and from work), it doesn't always work on everyone, so we have to improvise. Whether you're petite and slim or plus-sized with a large chest, it may be difficult to find blazers that will button and still look proportional. So stop trying to make it work—it won't. Just ditch the blazer and opt for a cardigan instead. These days, there are so many great cardigans in lots of different cuts, even versions with collars that resemble blazers. Not only does it follow your curves perfectly, but it also looks cool when paired with a belt in a contrasting color or an exotic skin. No linebackers here!

For those regular
Wednesdays
when you feel
oh-so-uninspired:

WINTER: Black
jacket + pencil skirt +
vintage watch +
booties + tights +
leopard handbag

SPRING: Striped
cardigan + wide-leg
black trousers + silk
tank + leather tote
+ peep-toe heels
or wedges

SUMMER: Silk embel-
lished tank + drapey
khaki trousers +
canvas and leather
handbag + high-heel
strappy sandals +
sunglasses

FALL: Tucked-in crew-
neck long-sleeved top
+ tweed pencil skirt
+ tights + pumps +
pendant necklace +
cross-body handbag

your belongings so you don't go bursting into the office, stuff flying everywhere just because you wanted to bring along your new minimalist bag. Wear a structured dress in favor of a drapey or flowy one—it shows, on a subliminal level at least, that you're pulled together. If the weather calls for it, consider a collarless jacket or a pair of crisp trousers that are perfectly pressed, a white button-down shirt, a pair of great pumps and very simple jewelry. (You don't want to be known as the girl with the weird hippy-dippy necklaces or the Pocahantas-like headband, do you?) After the first week, you can reassess, but you can never go wrong with these more formal staples. Now, do what you were hired to do: Get to work!

Champagne Taste on a Beer Budget

At the beginning of your career, when you're just starting out, keep the basics sophisticated, from your work handbag to your work sheath dresses and jeans, and keep your shoes and accessories trendy. That way, you'll be taken seriously but still look up-to-date—and you'll never pay too much for something you'll only wear one season. Oh how we wish someone had given us this advice—it could've saved us from having to eat all the samples at the grocery store until payday back in our early career days.

MOVIN' ON UP: WHAT TO WEAR WHEN YOU GET THE BIG PROMOTION

Wow, you did it! Here we are again, except now you're getting paid more, you're taking the measurements for your corner office and you've got yourself a new assistant straight from college. Now that you're one of the higher-ups, you must make sure your wardrobe always reflects your actual position. If you've been wearing jeans to work, now is the time to let them go. You'll still see each other on weekends.

Here are some ways you can use what you've got to make your look more professional while still being elegant and modern:

If you wear suits . . . separate them and see what else you can wear them with. No one ever said just because you bought two pieces together that they'd have to be worn together. See page 118 for the same lesson on bikinis.

Stop Wearing a Blazer
Every Day, Already!

We've said it before in day-to-night dressing on page 223—blazers can seem like magical pieces that instantly transform you into business mode. But that can only take you so far: When you get higher up the ranks, you've gotta change things up or you just become the boss who wears the same thing to work every day. Blazers are for beginners, so take our master class in dressing to be the boss by investing in these three jackets. They're cool, calm and best when collected so you have a variety to choose from. Bonus: They all look cool with jeans and flats on weekends.

1 **Think outside the boxy.** Play with shapes, whether that means peplum, utilitarian or feminine. Find your style.

2 **Embellish a little.** Don't be afraid of embroidery, sequins or patterns.

3 **Texture, texture, texture.** Try bouclé, tweed, linen and herringbone for some variety.

If you wear tights . . . try textured tights, not just opaque ones. That way you'll keep things interesting. Just ditch the fishnets, if you own them—they're simply not flattering or office-appropriate. Chances are, they make you look fat anyway, regardless of your size.

If you like statement jewelry . . . You're the boss, so you don't have to just wear the same old diamond studs—tell your employees something about yourself with your favorite vintage jewelry like a timeless yet distinctive necklace. If you work in a creative field, large earrings mean business, too.

If you like white button-down shirts . . . Try the same style in a new shape, like structured white shirt dresses or more avant-garde cuts.

EASY AS
1, 2, 3

1. Colorful cropped jacket **+** button-down shirt **+** ponté pants

2. Floral sheath dress **+** cardigan **+** pumps

3. Tweed jacket **+** slim trousers **+** riding boots

FIRST DAY OF GRAD SCHOOL

The leaves are turning, the weather is starting to get just crisp enough for a wool blazer and a pair of leather boots, and while those of us who graduated from school years ago are pining for tartan and an excuse to buy a fresh new notebook and a pack of pens, you're actually heading back to school. Lucky!

First of all, pat yourself on the back: You're furthering your education and we couldn't be more proud of you. (Well, we're sure your parents are a smidge prouder.) But we're here to talk about the clothes. Oh, the clothes! It's no coincidence that Fashion Week always kicks off in September—designers get that back-to-school shopping bug, too. No matter what your last school experience was, whether it was ten years ago or just ten months ago, this is your chance to be a fashion leader, not a follower. When students dress up, professors notice. That doesn't mean you need to wear a skirt and heels every day, but make a pact with yourself never to wear sweatpants or pajamas to school, please. That's the first step. Present yourself with a level of polish—your undergrad days are over. Here are some ways to do it.

Experiment with color, fabrics and layers. The most fun part about fall is that you can wear tons of layers and everyone can still see them because you don't have to drag your heavy coat out yet. Two other things you absolutely must have are comfortable shoes (flats, booties and flat boots) and a great way to tote your books and laptop around. We're fans of big leather totes (Frye makes a roomy one), and we can also get behind the backpack movement. Not the mini-backpacks of the '90s, but roomier, slouchier ones made of army green canvas or leather. You'll get a ton of use out of one and it'll be easy on your back. (We're guessing there's no chiropractor on staff at your school.) Not a fan? Try a satchel. There are plenty of affordable leather versions that will last well past graduation day.

You're not stuck in an office, so you can have some fun with your clothes. Get mixing and matching. If you're like us, you probably don't want to show up to class in lots of skirts and dresses—it's just not as practical for a student who's running around campus all day. (Not all of us can be Elle Woods from *Legally Blonde.*)

FIVE WAYS TO WEAR PANTS WITHOUT LOOKING FRUMPY

Here are five fashion blueprints to consider. Unlike graduate physics equations, these are easy.

1. Bright crew neck + Fair Isle cardigan + colored jeans + flats

2. Sweater vest + sleeveless blouse + leather or slim wax-coated leggings (seriously!) + booties

3. Silk button-down shirt + crew-neck sweater + wide-leg trousers + bright heels

4. Sequin T-shirt + colored trousers + leopard-print flats

5. Printed tunic + skinny jeans or leggings + skinny belt + flat boots

Pull your closet apart and start mixing a few funky pieces with each other to see what works. If you're a nerdy overachiever, as we were, you might even want to take notes.

Retro Glasses, without Looking Like Steve Urkel's Twin Sister

In recent years, there's been a retro eyeglasses trend in Hollywood and beyond—most likely somewhat inspired by the Mad Men costume department and the ensuing '60s trend. We've seen some girls pull it off in awe-inspiring ways, while others just look silly. If this is a look you want to try, whether at work or at school, it does tend to send a subliminal "smartypants" signal to others, which, honestly, never hurts. Add one more nerdtastic piece into the mix, though, and you'll end up looking like a cartoon character, so stick to sharp sheath dresses or, if you're feeling especially fashion-forward, even an evening gown, à la Grace Kelly in the '50s or Chloë Sevigny in modern times. It's ultrachic when done right—just leave the sweater vests and suspenders for another day.

GRADUATION DAY

After all the sleepless nights of studying, group projects, the parties, the exams, the papers, more parties and all that worrying about grades, in a flash, it's all over. It's your big day, when all your family and friends will gather to celebrate your accomplishments. So dress like you've earned the party they're throwing for you. There will be tons of photos taken to mark this day. Here are three classics to consider wearing so you're always in style, and can look back fondly, not in horror.

BLACK-AND-WHITE GRAPHIC PRINTS

Shift dresses in black and white, whether striped, checked or geometric, are always "in." Why not channel Audrey Hepburn in a pair of black sunglasses?

SAFARI DRESSES

Tailored khaki safari dresses are classics—they conjure up images in our heads of Lauren Hutton, who, no matter what the decade, is always in style. Make it modern with a gold glittery cross-body bag or a neon skinny belt, bangles and a pair of wedges (the better to walk in—you don't want potential employers gawking at your fall on YouTube). Bonus: Safari dresses are often constructed out of ultralight cotton or linen, which helps you breathe under that graduation gown. Don't forget to get some pictures sans cap and gown!

COLORFUL A-LINE DRESSES

This style is hands-down the most universally flattering on all body types. You'll never regret this look, especially if you wear it in a solid color rather than a print.

Stripes: An Optical Illusion

Our tricks: Wear horizontal stripes to create the look of being curvy and try vertical ones to elongate your body. Want to keep the eyes off your hips? Wear a striped top. Want to cover a problem area? Consider stripes going in all directions.

WHEN YOU THINK HE'S GOING TO PROPOSE

First, get a manicure. There are going to be lots of close-up hand photos. For that same reason, you want to put together an outfit that's Grandma-photo-friendly but still hot—to remind him why he's proposing, of course. All your relatives will be looking at the photos, so don't wear anything too revealing or low-cut. Also, you'll have these photos forever, so forgo super-trendy items that might be embarrassing in a few years. Try a little black dress with leg-lengthening high heels (tights if you need them) and your other favorite jewelry as accessories. An evening clutch (black or metallic) and a good lipstick or gloss complement the look. Carry oil-blotting papers for those photos. And if you've got anything lucky, now's the time to bring it along.

EASY AS
1, 2, 3

1. Little black V-neck dress **+** studded belt **+** high heels
2. Solid silk sundress **+** strappy sandals **+** earrings
3. White A-line skirt **+** V-neck top **+** statement jewelry

BACHELORETTE PARTY

We want you to have fun and exude all the gorgeousness and excitement that's bursting inside you. So don't ruin it with an ugly furry boa and a slutty dress. Try strategically sexy dresses, like cutouts—suggestive, not skanky. Don't try to wear this dress anywhere else but on girls' nights,

EASY AS
1, 2, 3

1. Cutout dress **+** edgy black heels **+** studded belt

2. Bandage dress **+** edgy black heels **+** red lipstick

3. Lace mini-dress **+** nude shoes **+** chunky jewelry

though—it can be a little too provocative for some crowds. And keep your hair and makeup simple: Let the cutout be the scene-stealer! If that's not your style, go for a trendy dress style, whether a one-shoulder party dress, or a chiffon and metallic number. Remember, this night is more about one-night-stand clothing—you'll wear it once or twice and forget about it. Just like tonight—it's a fleeting moment of fun and carelessness before you share your vows with the world. Forget about the place settings tonight and get thee to the club.

THE BIRTH OF YOUR BABY

Giving birth is not comfortable—you're already going to be physically restless, so you don't want to choose clothes that can be constricting, like jeans or pants. Also, you'll be examined as soon as you get to the hospital, so a loose-fitting dress offers, well, easy access. Plus, it's just one thing you have to pack when you come back home rather than a whole outfit.

WHAT TO PACK IN YOUR HOSPITAL BAG

A "designer" hospital gown is a good investment if you're expecting lots of visitors while you're in the hospital. While you're at it, you should bring a cozy robe. You'll also want to pack some makeup and a brush so you don't look like crap in all the pictures people are sure to be taking. If you tend to get cold, don't leave home without a sweater and a few pairs of socks. If you're planning on nursing your baby, make sure to pack a few nursing bras to keep you supported while you're in the hospital. Last but not least, leave the sexy undies at home and fill your hospital bag with granny panties instead. Let's just say it will be pretty messy down there for a few weeks, so you need underthings that are up for the job.

EASY AS
1, 2, 3

1. Loose-fitting dress
   + slip-on sneakers
   + cardigan
2. Jersey drapey dress
   + lucky jewelry +
   ballet flats
3. Maxi-skirt + tee
   + sandals

WHAT TO WEAR HOME FROM THE HOSPITAL

Again, a loose-fitting dress works well because you'll still have a little bit of a belly so the extra material will help hide the pudge. A dress is also a great option in the event that you have a C-section so you won't have to worry about fastening pants around your waist.

YOUR TV DEBUT

There are some very specific pointers when dressing for TV that actually make it much easier than deciding what to throw on for a cocktail party. First, stay away from solid black or white, or anything with small patterns on it. The two solid colors make you look like a floating head, while tiny patterns tend to give an illusory dancing effect in front of the camera. Next rule: Dress in separates. Since you will be miked, they have to attach the big fat pack to the back of you somehow and you certainly don't want those production guys to have to snake the wire up the bottom of your dress. Third rule: Add color. We were once on the *Martha Stewart* show and she mandated a brightly colored top for our appearance. A colorful sleeveless blouse (it gets hot under those lights) in rich purple or another bold, jewel-toned hue is a perfect choice paired with a subtly patterned pencil skirt. Just make sure the skirt is long enough so that it doesn't ride up when you sit down. You never know what angles the camera guy will end up going with. Throw on a classic charcoal blazer over the top to bring together the look. Keep accessories to a minimum.

Avoid jewelry that makes a lot of noise—and be especially wary of necklaces that will hit against your mic. One big statement bracelet will do the trick, paired with simple, elegant diamond studs to catch the light around your face.

We frequently see Kathy Lee and Hoda complimenting guests on their shoes, so go a little out of your comfort zone with some patent booties instead of the usual, expected pumps. They are versatile enough to work with any color palette, and the V cut will elongate your legs on camera.

EASY AS
1, 2, 3

1. Colorful shell + tweed skirt + cuff

2. Bandage skirt + fitted cap-sleeve top + earrings

3. Colorful jacket + silk top + fitted pants

BABY SHOWER

Your friend's having a baby, and you have to look forward to a tedious shower full of oohing and ahhing over miniature-sized clothing and diaper genies. (And the possibility they won't serve alcohol since mommy-to-be can't have any—that was our last shower experience, so much fun!) Since you have to grin and bear it anyway, why not dress yourself up in something that will make every other guest squirm in their maternity blouses? We're not saying you have to go all out, but a little flair never caused any premature labor.

Start with a simple dress in a neutral color. Then layer with a crisp, cropped black tuxedo blazer. Slip on a pair of fierce yet ladylike platforms—since you'll be sitting most of the time, your feet won't feel any pain. To add some color, look to pretty yet charming hoop earrings and offset them with an understated clutch. Then grab your diaper genie/organic cotton onesie/stuffed Winnie the Pooh and head out the door.

APPENDIX

WHAT'S ON SALE WHEN

Not sure what to buy when? We've broken it down for you by season—hitting up the sale racks couldn't be easier.

WINTER

Look for discounts on:

- ✦ Holiday gifts in January
- ✦ Gloves, scarves, hats and other stocking stuffers in January
- ✦ Sweaters in January
- ✦ Exercise and athletic clothes in January
- ✦ Winter coats in February
- ✦ Boots in February
- ✦ Lingerie after Valentine's Day

SPRING

Look for discounts on:

- ✦ Lightweight, transitional dresses
- ✦ Spring accessories like handbags and shoes in April—with further reductions in May

SUMMER

Starting in mid-July, look for discounts on:

- ✦ Swimsuits (with steeper discounts—
  and more limited selection—come August)
- ✦ Summer accessories like sunglasses
  and hats in August

FALL

September and early October bring serious deals

on end-of-summer fashion. Look for discounts on:

- ✦ Trendy fall items like peep-toe booties
  in October
- ✦ A variety of items, but particularly gifts
  and electronics, for Black Friday, the
  weekend of Thanksgiving

ACKNOWLEDGMENTS

I am most grateful to SheFinds' senior editor Eileen Conlan who worked tirelessly to make this book the best it could be. To momfinds.com and bridefinds.com editors Jeanine Edwards and Justine Schwartz who provide inspiration and input on troubling fashion dilemmas. Many thanks to our literary agent, Kate McKean, who nurtured us newbies through the book publishing process and came up with the title of this book. To our editor, Sarah Pelz of Harlequin, whose enthusiasm and patience are unmatched. To Dan Sackrowitz of BareNecessities.com who gave me my entrepreneurial break as my very first paying advertiser on shefinds.com and has been a great partner ever since. To my husband and business partner, Michael Palka, who accepts that I will always have three closets to his one. To my sister Renee who gave me much unsolicited fashion advice during my high school years. Finally to my parents: my mother, Jacqueline, an epic bargain hunter who I watched many times dig through piles of discounted goods for a prize, and my father, Raj, who gave me my taste for luxury, something he frequently rues when he picks up the bill.

—Michelle

I'd like to thank my amazing boss, Michelle Madhok, without whom this book would never have existed, and the very talented Justine Schwartz, who gladly took the helm of shefinds.com when we were busy writing. To my husband, Teddy Stofer, for tolerating my weekly Closet Clean-outs, which always disrupt our studio apartment but are oh-so-necessary. My stylish friends Janet Ringwood and Zoe Glassner, who are unfailingly there to help a girl out during the most epic Closet Stares, as well as Courtney Allison, Ali Widlak and Katie Hintz-Zambrano for their endless support and laughs. Special thanks to Mike Pugh, my high school friend and photographer, for taking my head shot and only asking for a bottle of Scotch in return. Thank you to all of the awesome writers and editors I've been lucky to work with over the years, especially Sarah Pelz, our incredible editor at Harlequin, and my former journalism professor, Dorothy Doppstadt, who taught me to write what I know. Thank goodness for my entire family, including my aunt Maureen O'Connor, who has been my New York fairy godmother, as well as my mom, Katie Conlan, and sister Sheila Conlan, who always let me play stylist with their own wardrobes—and of course, my dad, Mike Conlan, who fostered my love of books. Finally, to Nana O, who dresses up for every occasion, never leaves the house without lipstick and has indulged my inner fashion editor since infancy.

—Eileen

INDEX

Page numbers of illustrations appear in italics.